The Wars of Love
and Other Poems

THE
WARS OF LOVE
and
OTHER POEMS

With a "Reader's Guide"
and
"Lew Welch as a Teacher"

by

Charles Upton

⊕

SOPHIA PERENNIS

SAN RAFAEL, CA

First published in the USA
by Sophia Perennis, 2011

Series editor: James R. Wetmore

For information, address:
Sophia Perennis, P.O. Box 151011
San Rafael, CA 94915

Library of Congress Cataloging-in-Publication Data

Upton, Charles, 1948–
The wars of love and other poems, with "a reader's guide to The wars
of love" and "Lew Welch as teacher" / by Charles Upton.
p. cm.
ISBN 978-1-59731-125-0 (pbk. : alk. paper)
I. Title.
PS3571.P45W37 2010
811'.54—dc22   2010022149

CONTENTS

FOREWORD

DENSITY AND LIGHT

by Daniel Abdal-Hayy Moore

This wondrously lofty, Miltonic quasi-epic Fall-and-Redemption cycle, *The Wars of Love,* by Charles Upton is a bit like climbing a treacherous mountain, with some sweeping vistas and difficult crevasses, to reach a height that doesn't sum up nor radiate victory as much as intimate further climbs we, the readers, must make ourselves. It is a poem whose density demands both integration and eradication, sweeping up so many threads of theosophic, theological thought (mirror-glints from Sufism, some Buddhism or Hinduism, some Christian mysticism, held together by some good old American bardic individualism) and ultimately letting ourselves evaporate, through its mighty skein of words, before God's incessantly pure and anti-historical, even anti-creational (as *beyond* creation) Divine Presence.

Its classical High Church tone, lyrical by turns, works through ponderous calculations akin to the organ works of Bach more than to the drawing room melodies of Schubert, with some sustained stanzas of jubilant declaration, hitting the higher pipes for ecstatic thrill. Is it American or European, a translation from the German? Upton traces his ancestry through various emperors, kings and troubadours (his saving grace), some of whom (Richard the Lionhearted!) fought the very stalwart faith he now upholds.

Born in California in 1948, schooled by the Catholics, Upton's early poetry was published by Lawrence Ferlinghetti when he was a tadpole of mere 19 years, a yawpishly angry and visionary Whitmanic book entitled *Panic Grass.* In a fated coincidence, Ferlinghetti also published my first book, a psychedelic Blakean dreamscape *Dawn Visions,* when I was an old man of 24. Later we both shared another distinction, though totally independent, by becoming Muslim Sufis, Upton's path taking him through discipleship with Lew Welch of the Beat poets, and occultism (some of whose fairy dust filters through the present work), to deeper traditionalism and a Sufi *tariqat,* or spiritual path, of loving submission to

Allah. But the titles of others of his books give a glimpse of how we might approach this somewhat formidable poem: *Hammering Hot Iron: A Spiritual Critique of Bly's Iron John*, and *The System of Antichrist: Truth and Falsehood in Postmodernism and the New Age*. For this poem is formidable, even problematic—but so are Pound's *Cantos*, Browning's *Sordello*, Basil Bunting's *Briggflatts*, and of course Blake's prophetic books, to which this poem has certain similarities, but without Blake's prosodic transparency (but with comparable convolutions).

So what are we to make of this dramatic poem, with energies rising up in the forms of Adam and Eve and Unitary Soul redeemed, voices thundering and strong, sweeter strands weaving through from time to time? The work, Upton claims, of thirty-three years, taken up and abandoned, the poem moves forward in blocks of density and light, toward its epiphanic conclusion. Some passages of a strange beauty abide:

> Our real fear
> Is not of death:
> By the testimony of every ghost
> We know our mask survives it.
> What we fear most truly
> Is love itself.

Or as the God-Voice intones:

> Through your eye, I see what you see. Through My Eye
> On the surface of which your vision floats,
> Chip of wood on a shoreless ocean,
> I see Myself Alone. This is the rigor of My judgement,
> And My Mercy that overwhelms and drowns that rigor.

Later:

> "All hells are hells of the imagination,
> Because the state of mind that creates the sin
> Also creates the retribution.
> So remember God in the eye of this moment
> And stand free from the Fire.

[2]

And:

> The greatest beauty
> Is the beauty of the Invisible.
>
> There's nowhere to turn
> To take hold of
> Or behold it.
> (...)
> You find it
> By *being* the place
> In which you've always known it.

The ending stanzas contain a traditional Sufi epiphany of annihilation in God, and a vision of perfection in prostration

> ... *before the throne*
> *Of the Light which does not set.*

But Upton himself gives us a resume of the poem in a biographical paragraph:

> Traditionalism('s) ... criterion is the Human Form itself, as it rests eternally in the Mind of God, and the sacredness of Virgin Nature, not worshipped in itself but recognized as the many "signs" of God in this world, of Whom the "theomorphic" Human Form is the central representative.

So the joy of this venture is going forward, with the lamp of our focus turned up and illuminating both the whole and the islands of jeweled beauty that fall into its light. A call to us, and a proclamatory drama of redemption through vision.

It would even make a great ballet!

Fr. Rama P. Coomaraswamy:

"Don't start writing poetry now,
  it's the language of the gods."

Me:

"Too late."

INTRODUCTION & CONFESSION

Once upon a time, poetry was a sacred art. It was infinitely more "litur-gical" than we can easily imagine nowadays, and dedicated to a double purpose: Memory and Theurgy. As Memory (the Muses being "the daughters of Memory") it carried not only the chronicles and legends of the great deeds of the kings and heroes of former ages, but also the his-tory of the creation of the universe, its unfolding from the Night of the Unseen—its history, and therefore its structure, since the "history" of universal manifestation is that of a descent along the Great Chain of Being, the story of the "motion" from Eternity to Time—just as the *apocatastasis*, the restoration of all things in God, is the story of the re-ascent of that same Chain. (This is why, for example, we call our ances-tors "Grandfather, Great-Grandfather" etc.: in traditional cultures, ear-lier times were considered to reside on an ontologically higher plane than later ones; whatever *preceded* us in time was seen as having *prece-dence* over us in being.) Any competent poet would carry with him a vast body of lore, representing the whole spiritual inheritance and most of the technical inheritance of his entire culture, stored in his naked memory.

As Theurgy, poetry called upon the Powers resident on the Great Chain of Being, in the name of the High God Himself, to accomplish both the will of the Deity and to fulfill the needs of human life, in terms of mating, food-getting, war, healing, and *knowing*. Theurgy combined in one skill what later became split into the two poles of *magic* and *prayer*. (This theurgic quality is still clearly discernible, for example, in the prayers of St. Patrick.) It was prayer in the sense that it called upon God, to praise Him, contemplate Him, and pray Him to fulfill legitimate human petitions; it was magic in that it called up the deepest psycho-physical Powers of the Human Form, as well as those Powers residing in the surrounding world considered as the Shakti of that Form, or (in Blake's terminology) his Emanation, in order to shape and release those petitions, often at great psychic and physical risk to the poet himself. (According to Sir Thomas Malory, there was one seat at Arthur's round table—empty at the beginning, but destined in the end for Galahad—called the Siege Perilous, the "perilous seat"; no-one who was not absolutely pure of heart could sit upon it without injury or death. This legend led me at one point to define poetry itself as the Siege Perilous, and to characterize it further, paraphrasing William James, as "the moral equivalent of human sacrifice." The literary conceit of the Siege Perilous may in fact be derived from the Welsh legend of the stone seat on the mountain Cader Idris where a person, if he were foolhardy enough to sit in that chair over-night, would stand up the next morning either dead, mad, or a poet.) But nowadays we have magic without piety, and (too often) prayer without power. When poetic Theurgy broke down, the magical aspect became Promethean, if not Satanic, while the prayerful aspect moved in the direction of ineffectual sentimentality. And some-where between these extremes fell the art of poetry, which—though it sometimes pretends to magic and is often infected with sentimentality— seems no longer to possess the virtues of either prayer *or* magic; it has become purely "recreational."

So poetry used to be a sacred art; but when a sacred art degenerates, it begets monsters. That's why it is probably safer to practice the art of poetry without any spiritual pretensions. But I did not avail myself of that precaution; consequently I was forced to process the toxic psychic residues of forms of the Sacred based on archaic revelations whose informing spiritual essences had long since departed from this earth. René Guénon, in *The Reign of Quantity and the Signs of the Times*, wrote that

> persistent psychic influences, when deprived of the 'spirit' which
> formerly directed them, are reduced to a sort of 'larval' state, and
> can easily by themselves react to a particular provocation, however
> involuntary it may be . . . the influences in question can be quite
> pernicious enough, even when they are simply left to themselves.

Seeking lyric inspiration through psychic explorations of the "collective unconscious" is just such a provocation; I can attest to the truth of this from my own experience.

Central to the traditional practice of poetry in the west is the concept of the poet's "muse." This presupposes a male poet who draws his inspi-ration from a subtle feminine presence; some of the troubadours, for example—like Dante—composed their songs and poems in honor of the Virgin Mary (at least after the Albigensian Crusade "re-Catholicized"

[6]

Southern France). As is well known, the Greeks had nine muses, of which three—Calliope (epic poetry), Erato (love poetry) and Euterpe (music and lyric poetry)—relate to the art of poetry as we understand it. And given that the archaic Great Goddess overshadowed the entire Celtic world, it is clear that the Bards composed and sang for Her ears before all others, and by Her power alone (a theme echoed in the traditional Scottish ballad *Thomas Rymer*)—perhaps in Her aspect as Brigit, Goddess of Eloquence, Mother of the High God Ogma Sun-face—Brigit being analogous to the Hindu Sarasvati, patroness of knowledge, culture and the arts, *shakti* to Brahma the Creator: the Goddess of *Creativity*. For the lyric poet, the arrival of the Muse or Goddess produces a peculiar psycho-physical reaction, a spontaneous and uncontrollable hyper-ventilation designed to raise his subtle nervous system to the vibrational pitch where the words of his Muse may be heard and understood—*inspiration* precisely: the poet's Muse *breathes his poem into him*.

In the context of a living religion that allows for poetic inspiration and understands it, the poet's relation to his Muse is a conscious craft, hedged about with many traditional safeguards. In our time, however, the realm of poetic inspiration has fallen into the underworld of the "collective unconscious" where those safeguards are no longer available; consequently Brigit or Sarasvati has been transformed into Kali. In other words, to the degree that clear spiritual knowledge, emanating from the pneumatic plane, has become delusive spiritual glamour, residing on the psychic plane, the poet's Muse must increasingly appear in the guise of the Goddess of Death. The poet susceptible to infernal glamours is under the power of illusion—the central core of that illusion being his own poetic ego—and the function of the Goddess Kali is to destroy illusion; this is why so many poets, who have been left with nothing to worship in modern secular society but their own egos, are led to self-destruction: alcoholism, drug-addiction, suicide.

Originally poetry was both an art and a craft, two words that were once nearly synonymous. When the meanings of these words diverged, however, *craft* carried most of the original burden, denoting the acquisition and practice of a technical skill which, if a sufficiently high degree of proficiency were attained, might flower into true inspiration, after the technical aspect of the craft had become "second nature". (Any true musician will understand what I mean, most likely because poetry in its

[7]

original practice was inseparable from music, just as both poetry and music were closely related to dance—as, for example, with the tribal Africans or Native Americans. The prosodic unit of a poetic line is still called a "foot", recalling the time when poems were danced as well as sung.) But when poetry began to be considered more an art than a craft, the word *art* degenerated until it came to denote a work produced primarily through inspiration rather than craft competence, an inspiration that the poet could only hope would somehow bring its own crafted verse forms with it, directly out of his or her sensitive poetic soul, through which the "cultural collective unconscious" might, on rare occasions, find a way to speak. (How like the Protestant Reformation is this passage from poetry as a craft to poetry as an "art", a change that's strictly analogous to the breakdown of the sacramental order—a true spiritual craft tradition—and its replacement with charismatic preaching—an entirely hit-or-miss proposition.)

Poetry was taught as a true craft in the Bardic Academies of Celtic Europe. While the apprentice poet was learning *prosody*, the science of poetic forms, he was at the same time stocking his capacious, pre-literate memory with *lore*—myths, legends, histories, technical knowledge of many different crafts (astronomy, meteorology, medicine, herb lore, gem lore, divination etc., and at least the symbolic aspects of metallurgy, agriculture, hunting, fishing, navigation, pottery-making, carpentry, masonry.... poetry is built on metaphor, and every craft has a metaphorical aspect), as well as an encyclopedic knowledge of traditional symbols expressed, mythopoetically, in terms of images. He might also, in shamanic mode, become master of the subtle technical craft that would allow him to attain various states of ecstasy or "altered states of consciousness." Other cultures, of course, had analogous institutions. Persian poetry, for example—like that of Jalaluddin Rumi—also possessed many bardic elements. It relied upon a vast stock of known and memorized traditional symbols, as well as drawing part of its inspiration, at least in Islamic times, from the ecstatogenic techniques of the Sufis. (For insight into the bardic aspect of Persian poetry, see the 15-volume encyclopedia *Sufi Symbolism* by Javad Nurbakhsh, particularly volumes One and Four, dealing respectively with the symbolism of wine and of the parts of the Beloved's body, and with that of the natural world.)

Strangely enough, if any group in contemporary North America still practices what might be legitimately called a "bardic" craft, it is the Old Regular Baptists. Since they have the whole Bible nearly memorized, they possess a large stock of traditional symbols ready-to-hand (or tongue). Couple that with the ecstatogenic technique of hyperventilation-while-preaching, and a deep and pious faith in the inspirational and wisdom-giving power of the Holy Spirit, and you have, in the form of a traditional *ex tempore* sermon given by the hardshell Baptist preacher, or other preachers of similar denominations, many of the elements of the traditional practice of bardic poetry. (Allen Ginsberg claimed to have developed the idea of the "breath unit" as his version of the poetic line, a line whose length is determined by the poet's lung-capacity, like the musical line of a jazz trumpeter or saxophone-player—but without a doubt the Baptists got there first. And maybe those Black jazz musicians got it from their Black Baptist preachers in the first place.)

Under the bardic system, every poet was both the member of a school and the inheritor, practitioner and transmitter of a body of traditional knowledge—or rather traditional *wisdom*, a word that denotes theoretical knowledge become practical, information transformed into skill. But when the bardic academies of northern and western Europe fell apart, or were shut down, poetry was forced, by passive cultural decay and/or active persecution, to become an individual art. The broken academies released waves of wandering, out-of-work poets—jugglers, mountebanks and *jongleurs—proto-bohemians* precisely, who carried with them (like the Gypsies?) all the marks of a disinherited priesthood. (Who was Allen Ginsberg, after all, but a fallen rabbi, an unemployed prophet? And who is Jack Hirschman but a freelance Hasidic kabbalist turned poet, because he could find no place in his formerly-Jewish tradition to be anything else? The Hebrew prophets themselves were often the products of prophetic "schools", like the one on Mount Carmel—but as Simon and Garfunkel sang, back in the 1960's, in these days "the words of the prophets are written on the subway walls.")

So now we poets are forced to be individual artists with no stable patronage, freelances who must hope somehow to access an inspiration that we have no formal method of relating to, and can't even really define. And whatever our poorly-conceived "inspiration" or shapeless "craftiness" happen to turn up we must immediately pimp out to a public that increasingly doesn't care, or to the National Endowment for the

Arts and other funding sources, who will pay a tiny pittance to a minis-cule percentage of us to *act* as poets in their nearly-meaningless pageant of "national high culture". Seeing this, I gave up. I left the stage.

San Francisco poet Jack Spicer once said, "I write for the dead"—they being his only stable and reliable audience. As for myself, I wrote for an invisible "tribe" who never assembled; or for the dead, the ancestors—though it was not my intent to beguile them with my own uncertain talent, but rather give them a living voice; and, finally, for God alone. That's when my poetry took its true, if modest, place in the shape of my life; that's when I knew I'd finally been heard.

This book is made up of five sections: *The Wars of Love*, a short mythopoetic epic of fall-and-redemption, begun in 1968, substantially done by 2000, and finished word-for-word some time in 2006; *Thirty-Four Uncollected Poems*, written between 1966 and 2001 (presented not in chronological but in "dramatic" order); *A Metaphysical Commentary and "Reader's Guide" to The Wars of Love*, written entirely in 2008; *Lew Welch as Teacher*, begun in 2004—though I incorporated a lot of earlier material into it—and finished in 2008; and *Sufi Poems*, which includes "Nineteen Odes after Hafiz", transcreated (not translated) from the English versions of H. Wilberforce Clarke.

The bulk of this book is composed of lyric poetry, and lyric poetry was, for me, a struggle to reach emotional and metaphysical knowledge as if nothing had ever been known; it was written not by me but by my faculties of feeling and raw intuition seeking their own language, their own discourse and dialectic, on the terrifying assumption that my words might know more than I did, that they might be better fitted to speak than I myself. I would stumble across poems only hours old as if they were unfamiliar aeroliths still hot from their passage through earth's atmosphere, or ancient artifacts newly dug up, looted from some trea-sure-hoard, or heap of bones, whose exact location I could never fix. And so my poetry was filled with flights of lyrical idealism, what Robert Bly called "grandiose ascent" (which produced many poems too full of flame and bubbles to be worth preserving)—as well as the agonizing consequences of such emotionally self-willed and spiritually groundless quests. Through poetry I crept toward Truth through the grim shadows of that Truth: metaphysical irony . . . 'Gnostic' satire . . . all the regions of the grave, and the elemental caverns (all that Heat, Cold, Moisture and Dryness), in search of some form that might deserve to be called human. My poetry was what I said before I knew what it meant—or what I knew unconsciously before I really knew how to say it.

Ever since the French Symbolists, if not before—ever since poets began to turn to the lurid underworld of the "unconscious" as the source of their inspiration, as well as to the vision of the natural world as seen from the standpoint of that unconscious, sometimes via drug-use—poetry in Western Europe and America has increasingly become a vector for a kind of infernal glamour (Poe; Baudelaire; Rimbaud; Lautreamont; Georg Trakl; the stories/prose poems of Dylan Thomas; Galway Kinnell, etc., etc.)—a late modern phenomenon that is now in the process of being replaced by the infernal *glamourlessness* of post-modernism. In terms of Dante's *Inferno*, our culture has sunk below the sodden or fiery upper circles of Hell, and come to rest in its frozen depths. And on its way—on the road from infernal glamour, which is actually a kind of inverted Beauty, to post-modern deadness—it embraced at one point the deliberate pursuit of the ugly, as has been practiced by so many poets since the 1970's. And although this tendency is certainly still with us, it has begun to give away to a kind of post-modern, sub-factual nihilism, a barrenness of severed details unrelated to any deeper meaning whatsoever, whether archetypal, psychological, social, or natural. The "positive" quest for ugliness has turned into a totally negative *flight from meaning*, based on the very real fear that ugliness (since it is inseparable from Beauty, being Beauty's corruption) might actually *mean* something from time to time.

As for myself, I am a little closer to the 18th and 19th century English Romantics, especially William Blake, to whom beauty was not yet taboo (it's not entirely taboo even now); yet the "late modern" stratum of my psyche was just as subject to infernal glamours as that of many of my predecessors and contemporaries—a condition that I dealt with, especially in *The Wars of Love*, not by *believing in* or *worshipping* the dark dreams that beset me, but by placing them—sometimes via veiled satire—in their proper diagnostic context, much as Blake did in his Prophetic Books. (The *dramatis personae* of those Books often remind me of Blake's younger contemporaries, like Byron, Shelley, and Keats. The character-types, worldviews, and modes-of-sensibility that the younger Romantics seriously identified with appear in the satires and laments of the Prophetic Books as the elementals of the fallen Albion the Ancient Man, as just so many partial and self-deluded fragments of the Human Form.) And when metaphysics replaced poetry as my central way of relating to Reality, self-expression for its own sake was transformed into *diagnosis* based on what that self-expression had revealed—diagnosis in the hope of a cure.

My "true" writing—mostly non-fictional prose—is in the genres of metaphysics, mythopoetic hermeneutics, pneumatic psychology and metaphysical social criticism. It is written out of the psyche oriented consciously toward the Spirit and—God willing—illuminated by it. The poetry in this book, on the other hand, was written out of a psyche trying to understand itself without benefit of the Spirit, while unconsciously groping toward It. The psyche can never actually reach the Spirit, but the Spirit has already "reached" the psyche. The gropings of a soul toward God are really the darkened and inverted reflections of the God's immediate and total embrace of that soul: "Before you ask, I will answer".

For the most part my poetry is my only truly "autobiographical" writing, even though—ironically—it rose out of a psychic condition where there was really no stable self to tell the story of. The only way I could become myself psychically was to transcend myself spiritually, a work that is definitely still "in progress". Before we become ourselves, we are a chaotic mass of psychic material—hopes, wishes, fears, impulses and impressions. After we become ourselves, that established self is no longer "us"; it is nothing more than a sign, an effigy, of That which transcends us.

The Wars of Love was consciously planned as a short epic, a fall-and-redemption cycle like one of Blake's "Prophetic Books"; it was originally conceived of as a sequel to my first short epic, *Panic Grass* (City Lights, 1968). The central poetic influence it was founded upon was William Blake, supplemented by Whitman, Ginsberg and the King James *Isaiah*, and moistened by Dylan Thomas; but fifteen years of *tasawwuf* brought in plenty of Rumi and Hafiz before the poem was finally done. *Panic Grass* was my Apocalypse of America, *The Wars of Love* my Apocalypse of the Earth as a whole. In *Panic Grass*, referring to my plans for what was to become *The Wars of Love*, I wrote: "There will be time for world prophesies, when finally the battling directions meet, and suddenly are no more". For over three decades—between, let's say, 1968 and 2000, 33 years—I collected fragments of lyric inspiration, some of them looted from other poems and various fugitive collections, which I stored away, like pieces of stained glass, while I was laboriously building, tearing down and rebuilding the framework—cathedral or rose window—that could finally hold them. (And it took another 6 years, until 2006, for me to change maybe ten words.) The only way I could complete the archetypal scheme of the epic was to impersonalize my poetic persona, transforming it into the voice of Adam, as well as those of various other false "archons" and true elements or *hypostases* of the Human Form.

The *Uncollected Poems* in this book, or some of them, are a bit more personal than *The Wars of Love*, though the reader will hopefully discern in them an almost instinctive thrust to objectify all subjective moods and perceptions. I wanted to find out *what they were*, not just how I felt about them. And since I often wrote poetry in an attempt to understand and work through sufferings, inner conflicts and life entanglements that I'd found no other way to deal with, my poetry sometimes appears as a struggle against the chaotic and sub-human impulses of the soul, in an attempt to find and defend my human birthright. But since the conscious, spiritual approach to self-transcendence was largely blocked during my term as a Promethean, Self-directed, Romantic/Symbolist/Visionary Poet—only the grace of God operating through spiritual intuition can provide the knowledge and power necessary for that self-transcendence—I very often turned to a visionary contemplation of the natural world as a emblem of That which lay beyond me. But since nature is not God (though it certainly reflects Him), my attempts to embrace natural beauty as a substitute for God ultimately sent me down, like the English and the German Romantics, and the Symbolists and Surrealists after them, into the underworld of the Elements, the regions of the Grave. (This was the *katabasis* that Robert Bly, in *Iron John*, placed so much hope in—not realizing, apparently, that *katabasis* without *anastasis* is *damnation*.) My descent into, and redemption from, that visionary Limbo or Hades, the story of which is told in a more complete and archetypal manner in *The Wars of Love*, is recounted in a looser way in *Uncollected Poems*—which also form, in their own way, a "cycle", a myth of creation, fall, and return. And the cycle called "Seven Poems" from section IV, *Sufi Poems*, is autobiographical as well, though here the protagonist is not the psyche or *nafs*, but *al-Qalb*, the spiritual Heart.

In *Lew Welch as Teacher* I sift, accept, reject, dig down into, and metaphysically and imaginatively expand upon the teachings, both spiritual and literary, of my poetic mentor, Beat Generation poet Lew Welch, based both on the writings he left and on what he transmitted to me directly. In this (as in other books of mine, notably *The System of Antichrist: Truth and Falsehood in Postmodernism and the New Age*, Sophia Perennis, 2001), I show myself to be, like Kierkegaard and Savonarola, a true example of Yeats' *Phase Eleven*—"The Consumer, the Pyre-builder"—as described in his mysterious "channeled" text, *A Vision*, where he presents us with an entirely new branch of astrology based on the 28 phases of the Moon. I myself was born on the Eleventh Night, which means that I am "a half-solitary, one who defends a solitude he cannot or will non inhabit", a character-type in whom "one divines a quarrel with the thought of his fathers and his kin, forced upon him almost perhaps to the breaking of his heart: no nature without the stroke of fate divides itself in two". But I am also one to whom becomes "possible for the first time" (in Yeats' visionary cycle-of-manifestation—if, that is, he remains true to his phase) "the solitary conception of God". Bull's-eye!

As for my idea of the *metaphysics* of poetry, it is perhaps most exhaustively treated in my book *Folk Metaphysics: Mystical Meanings in Traditional Folk Songs and Spirituals* (Sophia Perennis, 2008), which—after I awoke and saw the finished work before me—I realized was actually a kind of *mabinogion*, a metaphysical and mythopoetic primer for poets, a poetic introduction to the Primordial Tradition. And finally, from my book *Knowings: in the Arts of Metaphysics, Cosmology and the Spiritual Path* (Sophia Perennis, 2008), here is a pertinent passage that expresses my doctrine succinctly:

> . . . . poetry . . . can be numbered among the final reverberations
> within the soul of God's creative act. Poetry extends the divine cre-
> ativity far and wide within the human psyche, both individual and
> collective; it carries that Truth out of which, according to the
> Noble Qur'an, all things are made, to its ultimate psychic limits—
> in other words, as far as to the threshold of unreality, evil and non-
> existence. This is the great danger of poetry, to both the poet and

the society around him, and the reason why the practice of it, outside of a traditional liturgical context, carries inevitable spiritual perils—as witness the alcoholism, drug addiction and suicide of so many poets in modern times. Poetry is the language of the gods. The poet, however, is not a god but a man—a man who has, as it were, stolen the divine fire, the ability to create *icons*, living images of truth. If his skill is great enough, these icons will inevitably command belief—not in the form of assent to clear and true doctrine, but in terms of the kind of emotional and intuitive allegiance that only clear and true doctrine deserves. Consequently, if the iconic forms wrought by a poet are not objectively true as well as subjectively convincing, he has arrogated to himself the godlike power to *determine what is true by saying it*, and perverted that power. Only God can say what is to be true; if a poet attempts to do so outside of God's inspiration and permission, he has become what Plato, in the *Republic*, calls a "liar." And this is a form of demonic invocation. According to the Qur'an, in the *surah* "The Poets": *Shall I inform you upon whom the devils descend? They descend on every sinful, false one. They listen eagerly, but most of them are liars. As for the poets, the erring follow them. Hast thou not seen how they stray in every valley, and how they say that which they do not? Save those who believe and do good works, and remember Allah much, and vindicate themselves after they have been wronged.* To *say* something but not *do* it is to extend the name and image of Reality into imaginative forms that one has neither the power, the integrity, or the *right* to realize. It is to create phantasms, to go into debt to Reality Itself, and thereby to wrong oneself, sometimes mortally. Poetry is boast, only action is proof; the poet who vindicates himself after having wronged himself is the one who has paid, with spiritual warfare and suffering, the debt he incurred when he arrogated to himself the divine power of creative speech.

This book is a critique of nature-worship based on the slow discrimination between psyche and Spirit; by it I hope to have paid a portion of my debt to the Ancestors, my ransom to *pitri-yana*, and so cleared the way for *deva-yana*, in line with the prayer of William Blake: "May the Daughters of Memory become the Daughters of Inspiration".

PART ONE:
The Wars of Love

NOTE TO THE READER

In two of my earlier books, *Hammering Hot Iron: A Spiritual Critique of Bly's* Iron John (Quest Books, 1993; Sophia Perennis, 2005) and *The System of Antichrist: Truth and Falsehood in Postmodernism and the New Age* (Sophia Perennis, 2001) I refer to a poem with the same title as this one; several passages from it are quoted in *Hot Iron*. It is not the same poem, however, but an earlier and longer version of it, which I conceived of as a "modern Gnostic system." A few copies of it are undoubtedly still floating around somewhere; one (or part of it) apparently did duty for a while as a "scripture" used by a Neo-Gnostic church named Ecclesia Gnostica. Some time after composing it, however, I came to the realization that the last thing the world needs is another heterodox tour-de-force by a spiritual free-lance—so I extracted only the most poetically viable sections, re-wrote them, composed some further sections, and so produced the Fall-and-Redemption cycle you hold in your hand. The "system" upon which the original was based, purified of its heterodox elements and its pretension to quasi-revelation, is now "The Shadows of God," an analysis of the universal roots of idolatry, the first elements of the human ego, which makes up Chapter Five of *The System of Antichrist*. Another branch of the original vision that ultimately resulted in *The Wars of Love*, which came to me at the age of seventeen—the part having to do with Creation and Apocatastasis—became an article entitled "We are the Bees of the Invisible: Physics, Metaphysics and the Spiritual Path," which was published in the journal *Sacred Web* 6 in the year 2000.

—Charles Upton

ONE

He who sings is a plucked string vibrating
Bound between two posts:
This perishing world
And the high walled garden of the King.

Only That One knows his real name,
And recalls it every day,
And in the canyons of the night
Breathes him as he swims,
Fighting upstream to the source of his
> *hunger,*
A flashing salmon in the black river
> *of dreams.*

Searching earth and fire for your Name,
> *Beloved,*
For your breast rising and falling in sleep
He follows the wake of your Word
On the face of your Ocean:
She whose waves
Have never stopped moving him
In the paths of this house of dust.

⊕

Never. You never came into existence. You stayed wound in self-ken,
  lapped in Your own delight.
Ships were sent out from Your harbor at midnight, but never found
  You.
There was no breach in Your courtesy; no guest was turned back from
  Your door.
Only I, of all your companions, was sent away empty.
I adopted Your own method then. I shared your impassiveness. I was
  as annihilated in the heart of You

As You had ever been.
I heard your suitors singing and pleading in the alley behind Your
    balcony;
I heard the heedless drunkards
Pounding at Your door.

So when first dawn broke over the waiting sea, the black dividing-line of
    the horizon
Left us in peace, careful not to remind us
Of something we might forget
If our vigilance ever faltered, distracted for a moment
By the cry of a bird.

Then the cry broke. The image of the rising sun in the world ocean
Shattered into a million sparks, under a seething wind,
Till every spoken word declared its separate existence,
Remembering quite clearly how it had been spoken by You,
Whose silence was never kept, and never broken.
No-one left You when the world was made. None were excluded, none
    arrived.
Your hospitality was perfect.

⊕

I am Your secret; You are mine. We never told it.
The long ages waited and suffered to learn that secret
— cry of the Eagle never given above the listening sea —
Only to discover that they themselves *were* the secret,
And that You alone were privy
To the script buried in the breath, rising and falling through the
    checkerboard of nights and days,
Opening Your eyes, and then closing them, on the kingdom of sleep
Where the roar of Your risen hand silences time,
And the perfume of Your Name
Brings news from the Garden.
I am your Face within you. You gazed on that Face, before the beginning,

without me.

I was the widening echo of Your Name
Over the virgin waters, when you knew yourself One Form, human and
    more-than-human,
Blazing like the Sun with archangelic rays, the ranked fountains of Power
    incandescent with knowledge of You, pouring motionless from your
    burning Core
Then shooting up all around You, trees whose limbs are conscious aeons
    and living numbers, eternal fixed dimensions and histories cut in
    crystal,
Whose branches are the swift messengers, signatures of fire, pages of
    the shifting rock-face breathing and moving,
Whose blossoms are galaxies and starclusters, the herds of deep ocean
    gliding like mountains, bird-nations exploding from the lake in a
    storm of their own language,
Thunder of bison across the plains
Of Your ancient and open hand,

All humbling themselves to know You,
Offering breath and meat and name as sacrifice to their Creator,
To be the seeds of tongues and laws, rites and doctrines,
Bricks in the walls of the human city,
Where the secret names of all things,
The stars standing in wait from the beginning
Pour themselves, willingly,
Red blood leaping from severed arteries,
Into the crucible of the Human Form.

See now the making of a Man! Watch, in this man-making, how the
    universe itself is unfolded
From the secret place. Your mother is purest water
In the womb of My being; My Spirit moves on the face of her
To write the Name of Unity
On the white scroll of your heart. And the fish of every sea
Will rise to that bait,
Because you are the gathered hunger of all things
To suffer human form, and employ human speech

Only to pronounce that single Name: *Allah*—
Word of their origin
Gone home in fire.

⊕

Can eternity deepen? Can God become more God than yesterday?
Where there is no tomorrow, how can the sleepless Eye awaken from its
    sleep?
And what wall can stand unshaken in that House
Where rock is wind and light is sliced in planes like a diamond
To stop eternity from deepening on the End of all things
Who rests without end?

Love cannot grow and must grow. My knowledge of You must fight to
    the Heart of You
Till You obey my command and cry my name and make me real to know
    You.
I want to shake my living name from Your lips—but Your knowledge of
    me is finished already, and mine of You—only endless.
The carven smile by which You know and accept

                              all that I am,

  Before I speak or breathe or

                    lift my hand

  Drives me from Your door.

                  I want the sweetness of love, and the
  bitterness of it:
             I want the trophies of War.

Because when I asked You
How perfect love could grow and perfect knowledge deepen, Your
    answer was:
                Through absence.

Your knowledge of Your Black Essence is deepening in Your own eter-
    nity, without motion or passage,

[22]

And this is Your withdrawal from us, the momentary distracted glance
That burst a cosmos of stars through the eye of a needle, and sent them
    on their journey, across an ever-widening distance,
The light of them reddening, bleeding, like memory itself,
To the final borders of space and time....

The Universe is the autumn of God, embroidered curtain
Closed on the balcony... and when You, Who demanded
    nothing, bowed to my demand
That You send me away to suffer and die and win
The proofs of love,
I felt only Your rejection;
(When we complain of Your decrees
The memory of that first generosity
Puts us all to shame.)

Then You threw me into a magic sleep, and cut me open,
And drew the world from my side,
Radiant, veiled as a bride, in all the beauty of Your Names;
But I could not meet her price. The seething ocean
Took her image.
And the covenant we made was this: That the day I remembered her,
And spoke her name,
And gathered her from the face of all things—
She who left at dawn to become my world, came home at twilight to be
    my soul—
You would also remember me,
And acknowledge my struggle,
Standing at Your threshold,
Victorious and wounded,
Obedient to Your command.

TWO

When God looked down at the Earth He had just then made,
It opened, like an eye. Adam and Eve stood that day
On a ground without memory—an Earth which did not contain
  within it
The bones of the human dead.

Adam was a word of God, striding through Eden;
In Eve God lay, and listened. Inside his heart Adam saw
The names of the Creator engraved on the guarded tablet;
Before his eye in the body of Eve he saw the shapes of his children,
  struggling to be born, and named them out—fish and animals and
  birds, mountains and stars—into the cold outer air.
From that day, Adam and Eve walked on the earth as human gods,
  through a world they carved together out of Space with the crossed
  rays of their vision.
All things were mirrors to them: the lichen-studded rocks and bones of
  their ancestors,
Shaggy tree-lords and the dark herds of ocean,
The magnetic cyclone of the frigate-birds above a sunken world,
Roots of volcanoes echoing the thunder of the stars,
The animal faces of their own organs and kingdoms under the Eagle's
  gaze—
And the shapes of their own names—Adam and Eve, herm and
  dolmen—
Stalking the forests of each other's vision. Where their two visions
  crossed
Was Eden. Where they forked
Was dark self-love. The widening circles of God's creative Wind
Crossing the ocean of cosmos, the face of the mirror,
Shattered the disk of the Sun into rippling snakes
And seeded the dream-universe.
A ghost of Eve took shape in Adam's eye;
A memory of Adam stood hard in the eye of Eve,
The Beasts of the Four Quarters.

That's when we all began to dream each other,
Till our children became like a swarm of bees in the green shadows of
    the pool,
Field of warm, buzzing energy on the borders of sleep.

⊕

Eve dreamt that she wandered East, toward the Gates of Birth,
Till she reached Eden's boundary. All beyond that gunmetal-blue line
Was grey, shifting ocean. She heard the Sea-beast call her name.

"Mother!" she cried. "When did I lose you? How could I have forgotten
    you? I can't remember—

It was on a beach somewhere; I remember now; I fell asleep in the sand
    and dreamt you were a whale;
You sank below me, miles down; I cried; I couldn't find you."
(And while she lay, weeping and demanding, on the shores of non-entity,
The Land-beast rose inside her, occupying the stations of her spine, the
    desert strongholds,
Red flickering torches on a moonless night. . . .)

⊕

Adam, in a separate dream, bit into an apple, and tasted blood.
He called Eve's name. The cry rose above him, his words like iron birds.
They solidified into the ashen face and frozen beard of the Alien God,
    hooded eagle on his wrist, tongues of flame licking the empty sockets.

Adam stumbled in his dream. His shield was broken.
He crept westward toward the Gates of Death—
And the outer darkness poured in upon him,
Beat against his named and defended image like a torrent of birds,
All grasping claws and stabbing beaks.
He was beaten to his knees, and so lifted his eyes to his father Memory,
    the Alien God.

[25]

A crushing weight of stone, carved with the fixed runes of history
Settled on the crown of his skull.

Then he rose from death in Eden, and walked East
through the shadow of death, in a pouring dream, toward the arms
of his beloved,
Head still spinning from the stroke of the double axe.
(The crack of the hunter's rifle called up blackbirds in a cloud;
Their song, like a turning wheel.)

⊕

Eve looked up. She rose, in her dream, from the face of the waters,
And called Adam home to her out of the bloody, dying West—
But what rose to that call, and advanced to meet her, like a walking tower,
a moving cliff, a tree burnt out by lightning
Was not a man, nor did it have the smell of a man.
She called her beloved's name and started a black crag walking.
It stood before her; impenetrable, aloof.
She touched it, caressed it; she wept to make it animal, make it human:
Cold unresponsive stone
Cast back her echo.

Then she died against the face of it, over and over again, in the autumn of
every year
To become the flesh of the crabbed and shrunken
World we know.

⊕

I have laid the foundation of my house, said Adam,
On a sand the Book says is the devil's sand.
My premises move and slide under my feet.
I have planted my seed in a plot where the furrows shift,
Raking the sprouting stems left and right. . . .
This cavern or grotto, shouldered by the green tide,
Echoes with the moaning of whales, the herds of ocean rippling like wheat,

[26]

Fish speaking in the click of rock,
Language hammering the dumb shore.
My story, my mirror's cherished profile—him I'd leave behind gladly,
    in a casket of words —
He has found neither home nor work.
He wanders from field to field of abstract merchandise, visions sown
    in him against his will,
Reaped without his knowledge.
He drowns, or I drown;
He drowns in me, or I in his flotsam, his carrion;
We go down struggling like brothers into deep Ocean . . . groans of fish
    bleeding from cut bellies....
Their diamond skulls, sunken treasure, roll down the submarine cliff
Into a deeper grave, or origin-pit,
Wrapped in a deeper word.
Not glowing skulls but shining babies dream there,
Give throat-birth to their spoken words
Like silver fish. And I—(Fool!)—I listen
To every one of them. My language is infused, infested
With the begged-for broken detritus of birth and death,
The black tetragrammaton, the four nucleic acids,
Of babies slaughtered for bardic power.
Cattle, Bison, Deer, Pig, Antelope,
Five species, five languages,
Bound through an atmosphere of water;
Heaving the shoulder of their silent Wave against me;
Drinking my breath.

⊕

The sands, said Eve,
Are those of North Africa. Only the wind distributes
The numerals that compose me, the arid glyphs. Plough and furrow
Died five thousand years ago in these valleys.
The rock of my mountains
Holds the fine bones of fish in silent memory.
I wait for the promise to be fulfilled,

[27]

My husband gone so long ago, on his journey to draw water
From the Wells of Aquarius. He said a star would point the way.
Who has seen him? Who gathered news of his troubles?

Where is my husbandman, my beloved?
Where is the rain?

⊕

My name is Light, answered the Alien God: my word, an unbreakable
    cipher,
Sine-wave of white fire on black basalt,
An accurate graph of my structure.
The carved statues of all things,
All I forced into existence to make room for my guarded solitude
Hang there like shields, like arms of my warriors,
Seeded in my blind and
Ringing fire.
None can come to me, no one can find me out
In the house where I live
Because I live in the house of Swiftness.
Nothing that breathes has eye to see or ear to follow
The count of that fixed velocity, that nailed emblem
Of absolute duration; only by my sovereign Number can they determine
That I am who I am: the rational integer
That burns down all who face me
To worship and white ashes.
I am the incandescent Limit, light in light of which each one sees
Only his own puny shadow thrown against the world
(Each eye broken
In the eye of the Other),
Voice in thunder of which no man's word has power
Beyond the wall of his own tongue—
Because wherever my eye chooses to dawn, all speech is war:
I draw every numbered man
Into the ranks of my book.

(Where all silence is crime and all speech confession
The groan of molten lava is ambiguous to my ear;
The lower populations blow like sand, they heave and surge like water;
Hunting is only intermittently productive in the forests of the Empire
Where the seasons jerk and twist like a snake under my hammer—
I hold land. I station garrisons. I cut the Earth into leys and borders.
I distribute the fragments of Adam's mask to my legions, glowing chalk
    of the kiln
Cooled and hardened into the stamped coin of Everyman, my name and
    my image:
Till every man is licensed to whip his own plate of Earth, drive cattle into
    barns, brand his women
With the burning name of the Alien God, as duly financed by lawful
    taxation
To be collected in the coin
Of the human face.

I hunt whales. I swim deep into the sea forests,
Squaring the net of the law against squid and dolphin, sea lion and
    albacore,
Till the ocean is a broth of pain.
I transform the heart's watery canyons
Into the wards of a penal zoo—whole species,
                     Excised from wilderness,
Shackled, cowed with drugs
Stand petrified, like marble statues, bone dry and white under the
Faltering eyes
Of the Crowd....
             (They leap against the
       bars of their own faces, taste the cool
          water of their blood and are suddenly
                 docile and translucent.)

⊕

I would give these two eyes, Adam said
To see your face again,
And hold it between these hands—
That face become all faces now,
In a bitter storm of memory....

I would die to know you . . . relax the blade of my anger
In soft shade. Dream an hour,
Or a year. To lose this heavy body
Under dripping roots,
In the heave and surge of water,
The ground itself, moving
In slow waves. . . .
I would lay my bones there; I would place my eyes
Deep in your keeping, if that would give me the power
To see that beloved face
Only one more time—for an hour, or a minute—
Before earth and water
Choke this voice.

⊕

The thousand rivulets of my blood, answered the Mountain Mother
Are cool water over the fever of your burning body
Which lives only in my memory: The day I was striding through the
    Lunar Forests with Eve my daughter—we drew you, Adam; our
        hands were hungry—
You leapt out of yourself to meet us; you held nothing back.
                    So find her now,
In the shifting mazes of the willow or the spikes of the cactus,
Her face dividing into twenty masks, lost in a thicket
Of thorny arteries and bleeding vines....
Or only the brief ripples on a pond, the shifting mirrors of water,
    laddered in section, melting down cool into rock....

The trees billow and heave in the ocean of Air;
One limb sprouts a fish, another a rooster's head;

A third puts out a gnarled, human hand. Earth-phallus mushrooms,
    flecked with seed,
Your belly sucked out thin and white in the
Trickling channels of my form,
The day I wed the forest tree-high, walking in bridal white and
    smooth black skin....
All husbands were my husband then, all sons my son—remember?

(The ice of your lips on my lips, said Adam, is not cold; it has no
    temperature; it burns like phosphorus.
"And shall I take off my clothes?"
                            Yes.

    "Fine, and this too?"
                   Yes.
                        We nod to the Kings and Queens
    of my spine as they rise;
It is a salt minuet, a courtly dance. We sway to the hammer-blows
    of Silence raining down.)

I am a silent flare of Power over a wilderness of mountains, over
    deserts of snow;
I am hammered silver, clotted ash, gullies of frozen light;
My devotees I leave exposed in lightningflash, breathless and
    panting to step toward heaven;
I am breath of their breath, power of their eyes;
They are nothing but a story retold
Over and over again in the slow circle of my beauty.
I look down quietly on all nakedness, exposing the lovers in their
    beds of seed;
I whisper destinies into the germ plasm and the budding embryo,
Predicting and dictating the count and pattern of the breath,
Done as recorded in the starry college of the midnight sky,
A zoo of glyphs and runes.
I am the terror that comes in the night,
Terror of the mouse, waiting for the owl to cover her, glowing
    faintly violet in the darkness;
I am the cool white nurse with her tray of simples,

Bending over the whirlpool that turns on the bed;
I hold the key to the citadel of electroshock—the roaring white
　　Silence
That wipes out all memory of the crime.

⊕

You were my flesh, Adam said—
Then that flesh was taken from me.

What did I care
For the dead meat left,
This useless anchor
That sold me into the power of gravity,
When all I wanted was to fly,
To leave this place
As you had left it?

I could travel anywhere, easily,
Any point of the compass
And never find one clear sheet of water
To return my face to me....

And when I tried to die to get you back,
When I returned from my journey
To the edge of this world and the
Blank white face of death,

My own body
No longer welcomed me home.

⊕

You were my burning Sun, said Eve,
But then that sun was darkened.
What could fire mean to me now,
When my thighs and breasts could no

longer bask
In the light of your voice?

All I wanted was to sink,
To bury myself deeper in my own
Stunned body,
As you had buried yourself
In the impenetrable sky.

I could travel through the whole Earth
    in serpent-form, that was in my power,
On in the form of woody roots twist
    myself deeper—

But where is the Sun that might unlock my
    heart-knowledge—
Or is he dead forever?

I struggled to lift the whole Earth,
Hundreds of miles of olivine mantle
Above my molten core,
And the granite above that—

But fell back
Under the weight of your absence.

The orbit of a cinder around a
Dead star is the
Road I travel,

Through abandoned cities of
Space and time.

⊕

I called upon her
She was not receiving;

She had other business
Behind the door of death.

I said I love you—
She did not answer;
She had pressing business there
 Her ear was deaf.

I died to know her
She was glad receiving;
She knew my voice and she
Knew my eyes;

I held her closely
We two were one there;
My voice was softened, earth
Choked my cries.

⊕

Our real fear
Is not of death:
By the testimony of every ghost
We know our mask survives it.
What we fear most truly
Is love itself.
—because there is a trance in death.
You faint at one point, they say....
And then all fear and hunger
Are equal.

But in love,
Death only sharpens everything.
Blood grows in radiance.
Every sense is clarified,
Every faculty enlightened.
The fluted mask

Of the face is shattered.
You watch—having no longer any way
    to close your eyes—
How every cell in your body
Is exquisitely, mercilessly
Brought to birth.
Oblivion does not guard this gate
As it does the gate to the womb;
The chest is torn open,
And what rises to the eyes, black and red,
Like water rising in a broken ship
Is not sleep—it is Light. Death
Is only a precarious, temporary refuge
From a light like that.
The soul runs from tomb to tomb,
Praying for a little shelter,
Pounding on stone slabs with
    fists of air—
And how deaf they are, with their
    carved smiles,
With their beards of moss.
A blind hawk does not escape the dawn:
He suffers it. Hell
Is the measure of resistance;
A loving hand, laid on breast or shoulder
The measure of defeat.

⊕

Who will write the history
Of the post-human age
The days we occupy,
When human flesh was only an unsettled
    memory
Nagging the archives?

Who will name the thing that so profoundly

terrified us
That we begged to be made machines of
To hide from the face of it?

                                          (I will:
It was *love*).

There is no home for us now
      say the sons of Hawking, the wise of this world
                        but endless space, the Dark
Mother—
      (We are *contained* in Her, sunk in black,
                              swarming emptiness—
      Can't you feel it?
      Our conceptual universe "finite yet unbounded" now,
            like the womb is, which means
That we haven't even been born yet—
      We are still INSIDE Her, held within
            invisible walls of Cosmos.
      We wander down roads of our Mother,
            through gales of energy,
            past galaxies of stars, longing
                  with the deepest powers of matter itself
      to break the light barrier, to reverse the flow of time....
            we are groping, stumbling back to our childhood in
                              vast Machines,
            into the Black Hole, the concentrated
                  Hunger of space—

                        BACK—

      before birth—

                  before spacetime unfolded its flower—

into a Bardo of buzzing Energy—

                  KALI!

                        KALI!

⊕

You who were never born and will never die,
Who stand in your high tower and look out
Over the lands and cities of Your own eternity,
How can You understand us here, nagged by the shadow of death, in
  mortal space and time?

You *are* that; you are My knowledge of you.

You Who are made of nothing but the bliss of Your own nature, and
  know that bliss as Truth,
What can You know of our great suffering here? How can You feel our
  pain?
What can You understand of an incandescent cloud of human souls over
  Hiroshima, ovens of holocaust smelting a fine ash of bone in the
  alchemy of Antichrist,
Of Timur the Lame and his mountain of human eyes?

You *are* that; you are My knowledge of despair and agony.

You Who are made of nothing but the Truth of Your own nature, and
  know that Truth as bliss,
What can You understand of lies and illusions? Whatever is real is
  purely Yourself; whatever is unreal has never existed.
What can You know of the battle of Truth against illusion, of a
  knowledge that is not only Bliss, but also Justice?

**You *are* that; you are My knowledge of war. And your knowledge of
  Me, that whatever is real is purely Myself, that whatever is unreal has
  never existed—**
That is your sword.

You Who know nothing but Your own infinite Radiance, Light that
  swallows the universe and us along with it
As if we never drew breath—what can You know of tiny worlds: a
  favorite street, a favorite tree,
A beloved wife or husband, a little house, a little child?

You are that knowledge; you are My delegated Eye on the infinitesimal
    mountains and plains of My existence.
Through you I know them as created; through Myself I know them as
    Myself alone,
Who devours the universe as fire consumes a forest,
As a rose-window gathers its fragments, magnetizing them to a new
    design
Of crystallized flame.
You know I create you only to destroy you; the clock you made
So testifies. Only *I* know that I create you in the very act of that
    destruction,
Ruthlessly annihilating the lie that you are self-begotten, tearing down
    the last wall that would prevent Me
From walking alive in your flesh, speaking with your voices and looking
    out through your eyes.
This is how I gather the galaxies and starclusters home to My Secret,
    through My Eye which opens in the human heart
At the command of My Messengers. And the pith of their message
Is that man never fell. You see yourself as exiled from My threshold,
    born into a self-subsistent world, a sky that doesn't know you.
Through your eye, I see what you see. Through My Eye
On the surface of which your vision floats,
Chip of wood on a shoreless ocean,
I see Myself Alone. This is the rigor of My judgement,
And My Mercy that overwhelms and drowns that rigor.
From the secret form of Man within me, whose essence is Woman;
From Adam the mystery of My self-knowledge
And Eve My veiled and My naked Truth,
The seven rays of My Mercy shine down into your mistaken world,
Into the belief that you are self-created, that the threads of your origin
    are lost in the wilderness
Of matter, energy, space and time.
My Mercy is Virgin, Torah, Qur'an: invisible sister, a lost world
Walking beside you, in daily and accepted sorrow:
Deep-forgotten vigilance
Spying on your sleep.
Remember Her—one death your whole payment—and I will remember
    you.

THREE

In the Cave of the Heart shines a hot, interior Sun.
Sometimes it is veiled by leaden clouds,
Sometimes by a mist of dull, tarnished gold.
At times the clouds are a muddy olive color;
At other times, the color of dried blood.
But beyond the veils of despair and complacency,
Of shapeless intoxication and grim spiritual will
A find gold Sun is roaring with knowledge
Over an incandescent ocean, heaving in mountains of divine energy,
The tidal-waves of the Aeons: passing as we watch them
But eternal in the Core of radiance, before whose face
We rise, and pass, like voices. Whatever word is heard in that light
Stands like a pillar
Between earth and sky.

So now the Violet Fear and the White Fear.
Now the full Beast driven from the heart, rising in front of us,
And us knowing him.

Open Hell. Seal not the door where evil dwells.
Stir the banked coals, the immemorial anger, the mirror-bound suicides,
Lizards on a red cliff at dawn . . . . they flex the sinews of their wings,
They take delight in their own beings. . . .

I say all will be pressed into service.
I say all will be required to fight.
The passive, the coward, the innocent will be trampled down,
Unless locked in single combat with Antichrist
In mountain solitude and stillness.

Invoke, therefore, the war in your marrow;
Call on the fight you were born with, that enemy
Whose lie is cut and tooled, precisely,
To cover your single truth.

Pick targets. Each man is alone with all men
In this night of war. The conglomerate form of Death
Stands guard on each human door,
Solid to the bullet, and the chisel—like those cliffs in the Sinai
In which our skirmishers discovered, still living
The imprisoned forms of men!

The sky is roofed with machines now, a guarded perimeter to block out
　　the angelic orders;
The earth is filled with the limbs of struggling giants, locked apart in
　　separate mirrors, in cold branching corridors of time;
They are powers of creation chained in elemental caverns when the
　　Human Form was planted on earth,
Because Man, when he fell, needed ground under his feet, the bedrock of
　　God —
But we have forgotten God now, and the rock is unsteady; our
　　foundations crack like parchment, they heave and shift like water;
The mechanical chatter of demons, the acid of shattered images are our
　　gods and our protectors;
The wasp and the locust advise us; the spider and the scorpion guard our
　　sleep.
Who knows this? Who has the courage not to worship
At the feet of his own destroyers?
Friends, I know you.
You are those scourged by what you see in the crackle and hiss of fire
That flowers in the rift of God. You have incontrovertible reason,
　　proof to silence laughter.
You are the face of the Divine Humanity, driven to the margins and
　　borders of the Earth,
Weighted and crushed by the Trust, till you release the burden of your
　　heavy word, to the pavement, to the center of the Earth if necessary
That the heart give up her dead;
You walk through the cities of the grave in the high mountains with food
　　and intelligence for your people;
You open your throats to the Messengers to give them a living voice;
　　saints take council beneath your ribs;
You offer your bodies to be the purgatory

Of souls you will never know.
You are those who in your hunger did not ask for food and so became
   storehouses;
Who in thirst did not cry for water and so became rivers;
Who in nakedness did not flinch under shame, but suffered it, rejecting
   the cloth of the world,
And so became a city for all people, where no-one is refused
But only those who know how to place their foreheads on the dusty earth
Can enter.

You live in that Year
When each man and woman picks up their whole cross and walks,
In the terrible sunrise, down the burning road,
As the structure of consensus reality crashes around us,
Torn free from the flesh of memory,
Stripped naked to Mercy,
Gone beyond Death –

The scythe reaps, the seed-heads fall
The harvest barn is hidden everywhere in the fire;
And the wedding-smoke rises,
Perfume of all love and murder,
Heroism, quite secret work
In the caverns of the heart,
Pounding the stone doors
Of those sacrificial priests
Who desecrate the Human Form to build the regime of Antichrist,
Gods of the New World Order,
Powers of frigid glamour, and insane false hope, and numb despair:
Pour fire against their sanctuary,
Against the Dragon
Against the Tower—
Glyphs of destiny, strung like nets
Through the charged structure of the thunderhead
Weave lightning into working knowledge,
Where the Living Truth sits mounted and armed
In the region of the Air, on the borders of the next world now shining

into this one, in dream and vision more solid than a rock in the hand,
To overturn their altars, those blissful devotees, worshippers of
    despair incarnate
To whom Love is a torturing fire.
At the precise point where their pain and loss are most deeply denied,
In the mouth of their wisest wound these words are engraved
White fire cut on black fire on the
Skeletal plasm of their nerves:
And Love is what we wish them.
But how can they accept such a gift from the likes of us?
How can they even know their need?
They are inheritors of the whole world—we are nothing
But inheritors of the earth.

⊕

So in the beginning we are walking over a half-barren field
That is the bones of the dead.
From here, God is a tower of fire—vines of light rising in scales of
    granite and diamonds
Up his thighs of forests and cataracts, tangled limbs of giants in the hills,
Studded with a million flowers, irises and poppies, vibrating in the wind
Of a precise and endless language....

His belly is the ocean, acrid with iodine, moaning with great whales,
Filled with the darting silver arrows of sentience, the tides of ancient
    feeling
That empower the biological universe....

While on the peaks of the mountains His eagles perch and soar, scanning
    the wars of His intelligence,
The burning white sky above, streaming with the rays of His hair, the
    black mazes of the night, the firing synapses of the stars....

And from here, God is a man and a woman, locked in pounding
    embrace,
Revolving with eyes and fingers, surrounded by the archangels of their
    children,

The Lion, the Bull, the Eagle and the Man, planets turning in deep space
  on a solid wheel of light,
Crystalline chariot of the Almighty shifting dimensions as music,
The living shape, in eternity, of the human body itself: a Wheel—
Where gulfs of fire and hurtling stones are succulent fruits on the
  Tree of Life,
Whose roots are invisible, beyond measure, beyond science, beyond
  time and space, sunk in the earth of Eden;
Whose branches, visible and invisible, are towers of vision, where the
  eye sees itself nowhere
But at the back of the mirror, among corridors of radiance, torrents of
  vitality, arteries of silence,
Fleet mercuries in the metabolism of God,
Whose word is Vortex, Star, Warp, magnetic Flux,
Whose word is Mouse, Bear, Bison, Eagle, the guardian beasts,
Reverberating from the fiery shield of the Angelic Orders
In Space and Light, Sublime Pen and Guarded Tablet,
  they who shield with their hands
Trembling human birds in the nest of the lone destroyer, naked
Before the vastness of God....

And SHE says: I am Black Space hugging motionless swiftness.

And HE says: I am Light pouring myself through space as music.

And SHE says: I am the spiral Void, the close grain of darkness.

And HE says: I am absolute velocity—step once into my river, you are
                motionless in the core of Radiance.

And SHE says: I am Universe, Black Rose wounded with starlight;
                my necklace of children is strung on a bullet's line
                  among these jeweled arrows of the Night—

I am the hunger for Truth, I know all: I am the Truth itself, I know
  nothing.
We are the circulation of the living Word, the eternal loud Cry
  generating universe forever,

Radiating our ancestors and children throughout the six directions of
     time and space,
From whom you've picked the loveliest of our daughters, the blue one,
     Spenta Armaiti, Angel of the Earth, to be your sister,
Bathed in the living furnace of the Sun—
Named her as Humanity's chosen seat in the six-dimensional signature
     of Eternity,
Where past and future, two rivers, empty their cargoes forever into the
     clear well of the moment,
Into a Paradise found, lifted from exile, held between our two hands,
Alive in the crystal chalice
Of the human eye.

The horn of remembrance now cracks the shell
Encrusted on the heart for six thousand years,
Awakening the nations of the human dead
From their iron sleep. The people of the tombs arise and have their say
On the plains of Akhirah:

                              "We are those
Who lie slandered under the name of death.
We have incontrovertible reason,
Proof to silence laughter.
From palaces of torture,
From twenty terms in the grey, damp, infinite dusk
We raise our voices and salute you,
Who still sit laboring in your dream —
You living men and women, clothed as we were
In the sweetness and the dignity
Of human flesh. We are the strength of your arms and your loins,
The voice of your living memory.
Speak us, man! Tell our story.
We've been muttering too long in our ruined halls, those narrow beds,
The groves still barren of our voices;
We've lain too long in the seed-houses, the uneasy archives,
     the crucibles of sleep.
Beware! The dead are hungry for those who will not live;

The ones who die into a coward's dream we consume;
We eat, and are not satisfied.
But as you remember Him, He will also remember us, in our chambers
    of darkness
Till the river of our endless dying flows East again,
Toward the rising sun."

The Giant of the human dead
 Now rises into the flesh of the Giant of the Living
Who awakens into Eternal Humanity,
All sexual music constellated, no human syllable lost —
His knee parts the Atlantic—he struggles, tears the earth —
He speaks with our voices, looks out through our eyes,
And his word is:

            "All hells are hells of the imagination,
            Because the state of mind that creates the sin
            Also creates the retribution.
            So remember God in the eye of this moment
            And stand free from the Fire.

            The seed of earth
            Is planted in the kingdom of dream;
            The seed of dream
            Grows up in the kingdom of vigil.
            The portrait is burned
            To give recourse to the mirror;
            The mirror is broken
            To grant precedence to the face.
            Whoever you thought you were
            Has no place in that court, and this
            Is the end of war."

            Then Adam, who is the Human Form
            Entered the royal palace
            And knelt in the Shadow of the King:

"Here are earth's treasures."

These treasures are here already; they have always been with Us in
the guarded vaults.
If they had not been here already, you could never have secured them.
If you had not labored to secure them, they would not be here
already:
Your work and your practical wisdom
Adorn our court.

"Here are the freed captives."

The freed captives are here already, my advisors and companions.
If they had not been here already, you could never have freed them.
If you had not fought and suffered to free them, they would not be
here waiting for you;
Your courage and compassion
Make our reign illustrious in every land.

"Then here are wounds, the trophies of war."

Here your wounds are healed—you never received them: Look at
your hands and your feet!
If they had ever happened in this world
You would never have known the honor of receiving them in that
world;
If you had shrunk from receiving them in that world
They would be here waiting for you in this world, every one of them:
Shame
Before the face of eternity.

"So I rest in your good pleasure."

⊕

No silence without truth,
No truth without speech....
And no speech without silence.
The mouse returns to her nest in the

            tall grass;
The eagle dives into the Sun.
In the roar of God's Silence
The speech of His heraldic beasts
            is heard
Exactly as it is:
In the heart of that Silence
Whoever listens
Becomes all Word.

The galaxies turn on the
Pivot of a forgotten Name,
Until that day

When the song of ancient starlight
Rises to the purgatory of
            vishuddha-chakra,
The lotus of the human voice,
And pours back our stolen knowledge
Into the womb of the Essence;
When by the Sun under our breast-bone
We remember the name of our Origin,
And rise, dripping, from the river of
            human language,
And start emanating from the
            Throne itself.

⊕

All things return to Truth, but not through time.
Each moment rises in smokes of holocaust
To unload its harvest of mercy or wrath, vigilance or
            heedlessness
On the shores of God.
Ages rise and fall like breath, moving through the lungs
Of a vast Human Form, printed in stars
On the black curtain of the sky:

They breathe in Mercy, and live;
They speak His Name, and die.
And whether the harvest is all the love and fear,
The labor and hidden heroism and secret despair
Of an entire planet, or the crop of a single instant
Of presence, or willed exile,
The scythe falls, the grain and the chaff are separated
Only in this moment.
We stand on the ground of Judgement.
Day faces night in the same sky.
Paradise and the Fire are near.

⊕

The greatest beauty
Is the beauty of the Invisible.

There's nowhere to turn
To take hold of
Or behold it.

Like a smell,
It comes from somewhere beyond directions.

You find it
By *being* the place
In which you've always known it.

Layla—that's just what she's like.
Her name has to be Night,
Because the light of day, unless it falls
On some mote of dust that
Thinks it has a name,
Is black as midnight.
Night is Qur'an—night
And all the stars.
The stars are the Book,

But night is the Mother of the Book.
She divests herself, when the recitation is ended;
Undoes the strings of existence
And drops it, like a robe.

When the lights went out
In the great banquet-hall
Where all the people I had ever known
Or ever would know
Were being entertained after dinner
By the two black-faced *fuqara*
Directing the spectacle
Of death and resurrection,

That was Her. Ever since that night
I have been a slave
Of the unseen beauty.

It is madness to cross the ocean
Looking for the ocean itself,
Madness to find a direction
That doesn't appear
On either globe or compass,
And then turn toward it deliberately;
Such things are not done.

But when night comes, and the wind drops
And the calm ocean reflects
The mazes of the stars,
Why not leave cloak of your existence
On the deck of the ship,
And dive, in your madness,
Into the glossy black water
That has carried you for fifty years
On the strict count of your breath,
And reach the Midnight Sun?

⊕

When I was a man, I had no Self but God;
Now I am the Self of every woman and every man,
One with all who walk the path of Nothing.
All those who have become Nothing before they die
Have no Self but I. I am the road the stars travel
Before the face of their Lord. I am a ladder seen in a dream;
Angels ascend and descend upon me;
My flesh is a highway of living intelligence.
When the seven seas rise like sap
Through the bark of the olive, changed into liquid light,
There I will stand, in neither the east nor the west.
When God summons the four winds back to His chamber,
Calling them each by its name,
I will be the body of that vast, returning sigh.

To visit God is to spend the night inside the Sun,
The Sun who hears and sees, without sleep.
So shed the world, and open the gates of dawn:
The Sun is about to rise for the last time,
Climbing the green balconies of Axis Mundi, the luminous steps,
Gathering in the fruit of what has been,
Storing away the seeds of what shall be,
Till it stands on the floor of high eternity, the Temple Mount
And prostrates itself before the throne
Of the Light which does not set.

PART TWO:
Thirty-Four
Uncollected Poems

The Lightning's Kiss

I

the storm is directly above us:
    boiling fog,
surf crashing on the shoreline
    of the hills—
      mingling elements
flashing white, blue
    moil in a turbulence—
luminous webs
    vapors streaming
      and blotting the Sun
and revealing him again
      in his course—

our external destinies
      rush to crazy oblivion
    in the sky above—

    here below,
      the Quiet:

    grey, green, dark & almost white,
the treetrunks boil up to Heaven!
    silver-muscled branches
  light up like bleeding arteries;
      slender arms and sinews of branches,
    sparkling hieroglyphs of leaves,
    architectural script of rock,
the gnarled old face of the vegetable Druid
    frowning thunderous from the roots,
      his countenance beating
      like a human heart—

and the creek is filled
with men's voices
the single-minded, the inexorable

in one motion through time—
rare fluencies of speech,
sparkling emerald syntax
in the masculine sunlight,
illuminating the brilliance
of contention and declamation—

sounds of crickets, secrets,
goblets of Egyptian sound,
moving downstream—

the linked syllables of Karma
talking forever
in the direction of the
listening Sea—

and behind me, over my shoulder
the Tyger growls—
chewing the bones of his prey to splinters
in a keening, crying Wind.

II

and the wind in the leaves
is the voices of women
wailing in love
or lamentation—
coiling whispers around the treetrunks—
drawing long shimmering cadences
through the five-fingered strings of branches,
and making an anguish of visible pleasure
that moves through the forest
like the cries of living violins
as the bow draws over the nipples
releasing a wind of singing
that shivers in the branches

and through the branches of my flesh
like ripples through a
shaft of smoke.

(exotic poisons:
      vitalities coursing
through rock & wood:
      the war outside
      by bomb, or dollar,
      is ground through
wheels of Nature —
      or Nature herself,
         moaning
      like this,
makes war outside
      this canyon:
      (the question
         should be: not
Which is Origin, Man
      or what he sees,
               but:
Where can I work—
      in these cool and
      harpstringed elements,
         or in the gut
      of the machine
made of human hands
      these elements see
         in their Mirror?

Afternoons in Wood

I

it is declared that there is no reason here
                                lost in the magpie summer
multifoliate forest
                    bulging in the vapors of time....
                                        Death sits smiling
on the pine branch
                    like a magpie,
                                his black plumage opalescent
like oil on rusty water
                        each feather bristling with a particular light
cry like an Avalanche
                    or only distant chimes revolving in the winds
of history
        that yawning gulf between me
                            and all I ever called my own....
vast archaeologies rise with morning
                                where green jungle fingers suck
at Holy Angkor's face
                    whole empires of the past
                                        here to change the
livery of summer
                where the cracked mission bell lies moldering in
the sage
        in orange Mexican sunlight
                            broken arches, adobe-colored,
remote
        dull glimmer, fading in the grass,
                                gone where the voices go
of animals too delicate to understand
                                pricking & snapping in the
undergrowth—
            and, far away,
                        under the shadow of another voice,
                                            laugh-
ing a dry paper laugh, dry paper wingstroke above

                                        in the sudden quiet
bright new blood streams
                          before Troy

II

from a languor almost below the temperature of the word:
                                        an epistle,
opening to you
              like a gaudy paper rose in two dimensions
                                        the very image of
distance....
                I sent it by doubtful & corrupt South American mail
across no-man's-land
                    to the home cities, outraged & crumbling
                                                    that we
protect as hard as religion
                            where clenched gray iron castles
cherish hissing red embers inside,
                                impaled on spiked fingers—
                                                    I send
this from my garden
                    kneeling on the cool plateau—
                                        I send this from
a certain total safety
                        that is sucking all the oxygen out of the air....
the quick electric insect radar is quieter now
                                        the scanner pauses in
the sun
        then continues on at a diminished speed
                                        slower in the heat
                                                    still
slower, still more refined in the sultry fever heat
                                        with a nauseating
reverence for the details on my hand
                                that organ of command in a decay-
ing household—
                the god-king at Karnak I am
                                        King I am

[56]

                                   without a country

I am

      excepting this dry land, even now spreading from my eyes

                                       a wide

land, where

        a few inches below the surface

                        in the white chalk soil

of this wide kingdom

              the delicate backbones of ancient fish lie asleep

neither dead nor alive,

            awaiting their excavation by one no more dead

nor more alive,

          one with a little respect for the desert....

                          the desert

surrounds me, white and yellow,

                no sign of a tree of a bird or of water

Ra lays his hand on my neck & speaks his heat

                     And the heat of Ra is the

only word spoken here

          and I am the King; I am the King.

                      my land is

perfect in its desolation.

         the horizon is empty

                except for one shape

one shape of a syllable

        a stark & hollow shape

              a shape wholly created

of one word—

        it is my Sarcophagus:

its stone shape has forgotten the mountain where it was born

        (this death
        this return

        later proved
        impossible

[57]

Sightseeing in the Late Twentieth Century

Saw the manfaced metal locust of the apocalypse in a
    twilight bus;
Saw a cadillac as a covered wagon trying to turn into
    a spaceship;
Heard angel's wings beating in the void, then settling
    on my shoulders,
 An emptiness purer than Space, like a cold and second
    skin....
And in the canyon of Yosemite, saw mountains majestic
    as dogmas....
And Tioga pass, the unimaginable masonry of Pharaoh's
    heads in stone.

Then Mono Lake, paleozoic salt wilderness;
    the Black Island a body burned by fire,
The White Island a beast in his skeleton floating....

Living spinal columns wriggle in the brine; worms with
    single horns on their foreheads
Advance toward me from a stone-encrusted branch.

And finally the pillars of salt, a crowd of them at the
    water's edge—
Petrified dwarves, relatives to those others
On the shores of the Dead Sea—warn me:

"Freedman, pilgrim—don't look back."

The Message Bearer

the messenger has no message of his own to bring
   he is a message himself
  starlight and earth together formed
     the bearer of consequences

empty of his own he carries the kiss from lip to lip
   from the gun to the heart carries the bullet
     and the seed he carries he does not own
    from the beginning of time it impels him

  he is a man become a message as the wind is a message
he bears the words of all things
     bears lupine and poppy
  down the hillside carries their color
     and their fragrance
carries the man to the woman and the woman to the man;
   he bears the brilliance of the morning
        and the heavy axe—

  in all he does he does one thing
    good news and bad news together
   the lights of Sun & Moon & Stars together
    he carries to their working-places

  as at midnight the motionless lake
    bears up the heavens

Alpine Lake

Alpine Lake, clear green bowl of time,

nearly motionless —

wind-rippled—

still—

a dead tree
stands at the waterline:
straight, bare of branches,
at one with its precise reflection—

till a dropped stone
turns the lower half

to snakes

Sentient Beings

The trees are seething
In the crucible of Air,
Fully believing they are not
Moved by the wind,
But by their own free
Impulse and desire—
Their limbs are shuddering tunnels
In the rocky cliffs of space;
They stand rooted,
Aware.

Sun & Moon

O Sun,
    I cannot look upon your face
    but a blue-black dazzling disk
    blot my eyes &
        devour all other vision—

O Moon—
    this evening, late
        you were dim at one edge,
    this morning, early
        at another

Poem for Ocean

In the depth of your heart
you say the Ocean
is There—
        then what is it
beyond these foggy hills
that you rest upon
and walk upon daily
and drown again in sleep?

Come out with me
From the death of memory
And look on the crossrunning
        Waves:
This before you is not memory:
This is a Monster,
Solution of your veins,
The real Ocean, crawling
        the beach,
bare-breasted and
Wanting you.
        Mother soon to be
wife of your eye, but never
wife of your flesh.
Too green. Too strange.
a tangle & maze of limbs,
acrid with iodine, moaning
with great Whales. Those
who wrote and sailed upon her
had to be awake enough
to spend twenty or thirty years
falling daily into a
single Dream.

Twilight Song

Evening turns
on the single pivot
of Terror —

light wakes up
inside the rocks,
bleeds back the sunlight
into the gliding dark

come home where the world
neither hears
nor whispers

but shapes of power
hanging motionless
in rock & hill—

sixteen blackbirds
on a naked wire;

where all the life-masks
unclose their eyes
into the cradle of evening,

till twilight
folds his hands & bows
to the first cool odor

of Night.

The Uses of Fear

"Be conscious in the air;
be conscious in the vault of sleep,
    because I am watching you."

In this way, a black, whistling man
coming slowly down the face of a
    distant hillside

    sharpens my profile.

For Dylan Thomas

A killing remembrance
He spoke as he departed;
He raised his cups to nothing but to recover
His singing flesh gone out on the tide.

A blood-red voice, wide-armed & sinking fast
In the black of night he was,
As he drank his health to earth and death
By the heroes in the flagon
He celebrated in their unbreakable icons,
Who so broke and numbered his bones
And cast them, branch by branch,
To the offshore hunger lying low
Between the horns of the sea
He sang, who swung him
High to a crest then towed him under;
Who rose like a wall
And broke like a tongue
Was named by the word of a Wave:
Dylan, Dylan, Dylan, Dylan
Now grapples moaning up the shore;
White under the Moon's full ice he is
A white wave dying back
Into the cold Ocean's bosom
Who was the Ocean's hot & bloody voice.

The Terror of the Eye

The knuckles of Elephant Mountain
   show yellow silver
through a haze of fog
   and Terror —

the eye's terror asking
  WHAT IS THIS WORLD?

—these shapes of Mountain
      and blooming Tower,
  human figures walking and
  fiery Machines?

The world is a vague
translucent film, green hillsides
  and grazing cattle

covering what flaring white
  shapes of Terror, lodged
behind the torn curtain
  of my vision,
  entrenched there,
     beyond attack?

Madness will never be the
  name for it —
it is that I am being *fooled*.

We have no choice but to
  agree to this world —

but those who made it
by hidden mandate of the Creator
     did not consult us in their work.

The human eye
  does not obey our desire;
  we are foreigners here.

Merlin's Passing

And Merlin was old among his books;
His battles were ended; their memory,
    heavy.
His head was bowed in quiet and
Dark thought —

For though Arthur's arm was the
    strength of his blade,
Merlin's voice was the song it made
As it mowed down his enemies like
    a forest,
Tricked, elf-confounded,
And stupid with fear.

He thought of blood shed.
He thought of his pact
With the Powers of the Air
And the languages of leaf and wood,
Of the elements he had driven
As slaves and warriors
In the battles of his lord:
Of that contract,
And payment now due in full:
He thought of Nimuë.

So he rose from the table of his craft
And walked out over the meadows,
Green and sunny in the dying light
Till he came to the edge of the forest
And the shores of the lake—
And there sat Nimuë, wet as a fish,
A flashing blade in the late sun,
A glint of gold in the mist,
Combing out her hair as the ranks of
    the evening

Closed behind her, and advanced
In the direction of her feet.

"Merlin, what was that story you
　　were going to tell me?
Please tell it now."

And Merlin, one eye on the scissors
　　at her waist,
Sat and spoke, for a year or a century,
Till he had given his voice
To the wind in the branches
And the chattering gossip of birds,
That there once lived a man who
　　could command the storms,
But Fool, he fell in love backwards,
And so left his woman mad and hungry
As this unseasonable cold.

And Merlin's Angel said:

"You were a man formed able
To deal equally with Sky and Earth,
With Almighty God above
And the woman your king fought long
　　and bitterly
To save and keep,
And who now bears the bones of his
　　knights
In a deep sorrow, a darkening upon
　　the face of the wood,
A red stain upon the belly of the pool.

"Broken power, I'll tell you a secret:
Almighty God was alone in Heaven,
And desired—in one quarter of
　　His heart—

That the world He made
Be no longer subject to Him as a slave
But an equal and a wife.
So he bent His head in sleep and was
    born from her.
Arthur He sent to protect her from
    tyrants;
You he sent to wake her from her sleep,
And to witness their vows.

"You have failed in that work:
Earth still waits for her God.
The Word He gave you on the day of
    your birth—
'Bring to the lost and abandoned wood
The heart and eyes of Man'—that word
    has lapsed.

"Fool—you have become the wood—
Now the wood is lost to you.
You used its powers for war:
Now they are your jailers.
Your face has been expunged: only
    your voice is left—
And that voice is as immortal
As a single drop of water
In all the oceans of the world."

The Teacher

He reached down, picked up a handful of sand, and said:

"In each one of these grains of sand is all the pain of all the worlds.
In this single grain is Famine, War, Pestilence and the Fear of Death.

and this"—

he poured out his handful of sand against the wind—

"is Joy."

Tripura

I know you better now, Great Mother;
You are not as they said you were:
Twofaced, a musky hollow, a triple maze,
Five voices moaning in the murky current,
    under cypresses....

You are, simply, the witness of my whole life —
Flame of the candle unflickering, motionless
in the wind of birth, in the wind of time,
    In the wind of death.

The Death of My Home

my father did not know
how to mourn:
and so an old sorrow rose
unexpectedly in him one day
and killed him
in the flower of his age....

so I went back with my mother
to my old burned house
where the trees were dying
and returning new in a human shape—

the wall burned out and opened to air,
the sky and the cry of the gulls and the seasounds
threaded through what was once ribbed secure
in the old days, like weeds through a fragrant carcass,
changing its purpose in death—

Twenty years in a monastery, senses refined by light work,
  mind occupied with a symmetrical dogma,
    angelic inhuman quarter of the heart fed with cut glass
      & organ chant
  all that the soul might be left free to remember the
      branch outside the window
  heavy with blossoms, and the patio of the trellised
      vines
    as they are forever at the first blessing,
      reached for by a drowning hand.

A Birth

Infant, new man,
I see in your face the memory of the
Storm you were born from.
Facing first life you are
Determined, impatient,
Frightened, and tough. Seeing this,
I understand why we forget—see also
Why we had better spend
The count of our breath,
The freely-given moments of this life
Remembering.

Love Faces This

Lovers, in defense,
   in blindness, do not know
what heaps war on their
    tiny rooms.

In the bedrooms and kitchens
   of apartment buildings
the conflict of the whole earth
    is bled away piecemeal:

and love is sold for breath;
and breath is bent to hedge the
    lie of money:

that every man is a whore,
   and likes it—

that every woman has been denied
    her right to be a whore,
but now shall secure that right —

And the anger that
in the battle of the day
   made slack work
and the thin smile of fear

falls, in the night
    on Love.

(To cry for forgiveness
   and beat it back—this, we know
is endless:
      So, my wife,
   let us bank that fire hot
against the cold rain outside,
and against the killers who may
   yet be us.)

The Hour of the Floods

Struggling upstream, through the fiery
blood of the sun, against the
current of a dying world. (Amber water;
the excavated heart
at the hour of the floods.)
                                    Struggling
among the legs of sleepers bound.
In murmuring file they pass us, easily,
walking the river like a road. Their
conversation light, and dry, they
float downstream under no pressure
but that of destruction. They have
forced me to see them as ghosts —
that is, as memories. (Yes, enemy,
I remember you: you have been
unable to prevent it.)
     Inch by inch
against the full weight of the water,
wading, handholds slipping, then the
firmer grip on a wing of rock, we are
moving so swiftly that those around us
whom we once knew are a
blur of speed. My wife, that you are the
only person in my life, now
whom I can actually say
that I *know* —is, for you
the most difficult fate imaginable.

And when we come to the shallows,
sore ankles bumping the cobblestones,
then out on the flat beach, heavy and wet
that's when we we'll see
if love is anything more
than the desperate handhold
by which the passage of death is measured.

(I do not hate those
who have decided to turn with every wind,
to obey, implicitly, even before the
command is uttered, whatever voice like a
slow bullet seems to be coming
out of the grey dawn ahead,
because I can no longer see them.
They have lived like the dead, and so share the
fate of the dead: to be forgotten—that is,
to be remembered.
                    Friend,
I remember you.)

Mt. Offield Lookout

on Mt. Offield Lookout at the end of day
I stand in the silence I have made:
clear blue sky against the black horizon,
a jagged line;
mountain range after mountain range,
as far as the eye can see....

till hot tears burn my vision:
this Earth—is so *old*—

only the shrill cold flutes of the Andes
have sung the true song

of this ancient and
fatherless Rock

Homecoming

The wide Earth, changed
from when I knew it;

the smell, richer,
older....

fragrant with lichens,
the rocks
simmer in midday heat;

word of the ancestors
murmuring
in this present breeze....

Behind the
screen of the liveoaks,

down the valley where the
hawk dives and the
buzzard turns in lazy updraft

over shrunken tendons and
dry bones of my teacher,

stand those white shapes of Terror
who hold this world in existence —

thunder-riven Giants
rooted tree-high
behind the visible Earth
on the *real* Earth.

Song of the Dust:
A Prayer in Time of Drought

A dust of prayer. Gritty to the teeth. Ochre. Brown.
Taste of earth on the tongue, scent in nostril.
Savoury. Salt.

Prayer. That the dust find honey, and nectar, and wine.
dust that has grown, year by year,
in the corners we refused
to labor to see.

Dust. And the end of our laws. The laborious details,
unrelated to the tortured body,
torturing it the more—but the sluice
has little time: the dry, Moon-pearly,
gritty sluice of the night
is almost
empty. Of dream-grit,
the dust of the heart,
burnt & pulverized seed, yielding an ash
to redden the eye on torment—almost
gone:
in the curled & empty
shell of the Ear: Moon-dry, and White, House, of Water
empty arm-sheathes rattle in the Call: call to the pearl
of the Moon. Nacre whorled in woodgrain
in the night between the stars,
and peppering with dreams
the thirsty sleepers: of dry hills, rubble,
decomposed mesas in the golden grass. The pine,
oak, juniper of another continent—
dry and clotted as the Moon. Water
is truth in casket,
and runnels small and threaded with
sandy deltas and moss-sided riverbanks
all over the thirsty Earth. What I deny myself

the heavens deny again. An echo, brutal, almost automatic
of the locked heart of seed
and water. Water, on our lips always,
that which we speak with, that which is called
by the scented and drinking willows...a prayer forms
in cracked adobe, knowing who we are
and what we would speak
and have water to speak with. Frightening
the way it teases the heart. The rain, hot,
and tormenting, like rock. Hard. Hard to open
the crystalline flower, operated on mechanical pressures,
the worm-gears of the
learned response. Hard to be touched by
and hold
life,
when the ear is full of nothing
but a lunar Flood,
a white silence of Bone, and Dream.

Laughter at the Stake

Where is my body so I can speak with you?
Once I had a body I could rely upon, a
    body I could speak with,
But it was only a gift. A house and a cradle.
An imagined playmate in a child's game—

Not such flesh as is becoming me now,
Burned to unbreakable glowing ash,
Reformed to the roots of its crystal blood —
Fallen blood—old black blood in the
    whitened wound
Is a delicacy now, a savoury egg or sweetmeat;
As a fat sealskin is filled
With the carcasses of birds
And left to rot & ripen on the tundra
In the clean cold,
                    there are Powers
Irresistibly drawn to this fragrance—
And I have no room for them, no word by whereby
    to send them,
They are the Hungry....

So I am burning now,
My arteries like incandescent wires—
And the black smoke billowing, thick with grease —
While the circling sharks of the Air
Crackle & die at the same leaping banquet
At which they feed.

It is a lie that Death ever wanted my face.
Those who have disappeared
Do not ask for my disappearance
Buy strictly for the light of this Fire:
That Death is not a hollow cave
Filled with words without voices

Hunger without tooth or gut to kill to drink
    & be satisfied,
But the free spread of Motion—meat & memory
    bourn on the same Wave;
The thunder of the traffic;
The spoken word which is Motion in Purity;
The swarm of a windy tree —

Moving past no point just rippling Cross- or
    Star-pattern,
Like the surface of a pounded keg —
Or the weedy snakes that lie stripped of their bodies
When the Ocean is removed from its Wave —
Or the Flame that laps this flowering wrist
And breaks upon this tongue,
That burns away all knowledge
And in this way speaks the Truth.
Show me the page on which the Final Name
    could be written —
It curls & burns already.
The Fire has room for flesh, and for books too:
The Fire is generous.

Time to Stop

Time to stop mistaking yourself
For the one who says he's you:
Saint, political theorist, new image of man,
Mouthpiece of his anonymous brothers
Bound in graveyard, locked in god-form,
Bones of his suicided teacher rotted dry
In some crevasse of the Sierras,
Still giving off their ghostly half-life....
Time to turn the mirror to the wall and
    consult the window instead,
To remember yourself in broad daylight
Matched against the shadow
Of the One who knows you're Him.

The Last Thing Adam Said
Before He Forgot Everything

All knowledge ends in ignorance,
    that is: All knowledge ends in
other people's actions, which
    end in money—and money
is the purest ignorance:
Whoever has enough money can
    ignore the whole world, so that:

if the Tree (if it is a tree)
    outside my window (if that is what this—
this—(what shall I call it?) is called)
    is called a "tree,"

it is only by the sufferance, and the
    ignorance, of those
Principalities and Powers who own
        "Tree—"
the word, the vegetable material,
the concept, and my experience
    of the concept—which,
in my moments of ignorance,
        I call "Tree."

Better be a fool with a bloody hand
        at random!
(if this is all they allow), than be
    blood transmuted
beyond gold, beyond silver,
    beyond paper, beyond number
who make this tree their accomplice:

so that every time I am called
        to know a tree,
I see the tree they have killed—

and every time I see the
                tree they have killed,
    it is only because the hard supply
      of gold, of silver,
      of paper, of number, now buys
  — by random doom of market —
            too little of my *blood*.
     I say this to show you
  why I start with a pebble
      of undetermined composition
  and of no known value: This pebble
    outweighs the world.

One Version of Enlightenment

I am an animal walking on a planet.
I am an angel flying.
I have transferred my assets
To cold white lightning in a desert place:
Now my wealth is incorruptible.
The black crow keeps my treasure.
The wind does my buying and selling for me.
My strong vault is the thundercloud.

In this house without walls
There is no one available
To sew together the positions I took
Before this or that master;
Here, each separate thing,
Living or dead, is empty.
In this house without walls
A thousand redwing blackbirds
Exploding from the heath
Are nothing but the motion of light—

Their song, like a turning wheel.

A Visit to the Stone Clock

Sun Moon and Stars work on wires, across an iron sky
Over bloody Stonehenge.

Wizards torture power
Out of known tensions of conjunction and opposition
To lay down on Britain
An iron rule.

They cry down the Guardians themselves, ground their
    massive charge—
Till ancient terror of magic sails along the lines
From stone to stone:
No mercy, only titanic power
In those sentinels.

May we never dare to remember
What they most certainly knew.

Modern Cosmology

Even in the day
We feel surrounded by the night.
In the universe bequeathed to us
By our instruments
The daytime sky is not blue;
It is black.
Strange to think
That the starry world is now
A city to our eyes,
A mathematical construct,
A political entity, with all its
Streets and underworlds,
Where day blazes only
At the throw of a switch,
And night is a plaza or industrial park
Where the sodium-lamps,
Humming in a current
Of artificial power,
Burn forever.

Zone America

America is a hunger
of meaningless pictures
and nameless men,
where nothing is given
and all is "available."
everything is possible,
my friend Bill once said,
but nothing is likely;
and when he said that,
he said America.

What do we possess?
What is our own?
An accelerating desert
of inhuman motives
in which rages a sandstorm
of *facts*—
where the hungry, depleted air
sucks the soul from our pores
and feeds it to the shriek and
    slash of demonic images.
A clear oppression, an established
    tyranny
one single enemy—
what must we have been reduced to
if this is what we pray for?

And my native tongue is dying,
and with it the names of my land,
slow words, tasted and savored
that let its hills stand rooted in the
    memory,
in human space and time....

The archives are shattered.
The treasure of all human history
is laid out on this table —
but what the arm can work it?
What the loin can give
Or withhold it?
Whoever would live a life here
worthy of the water he drinks the
    air he breathes,
must fast, in silence
in the sucking hunger around us,
till there is born in him a word
that has power—
a voice from somewhere beyond
the deserts of fading humanity,
and the gleaming cities of lies.

This is the harvest land,
where the weeds are burned
and the grain stored up,
this deserted highway,
this spread, this map
of ghosts and dreams....

There remains this value
—held, or wasted—
in having been
an American.

Voice of the Antichrist

Inside my own body, my will is law: I leave nothing to
    chance.
Neither priest's black book nor pale human morality
    hold the power
To bend the fixed rod of my course.
I purchase and put on the fiery image that gives me
    power over the stars;
I admire myself, when day is done, in the frozen mirror of
    cocaine.
Circumstances fall to me, and jobs, and sales, and deals;
I reap my profits, invest them in global empire,
Because man is made to conquer the future, to cut his
    way, by pure self-will
To the galaxies of his ultimate form.
The findings of impartial research reveal my word to
    have been inevitable from the beginning;
The future is assured to my flesh;
No other lives in my image. I cut out the impostors
With knives, with military interventions,
With judiciously placed rumors, with massive transfers of
    capital;
I grip the wheel of the stock exchange, aiming for target
    center with the
Weapon of mobile assets; the pirates of my right and
    my left hands
Come from all the finest mafias and universities....
I am without rival. The sentimentalized face of God the
    Father
I have limited to residual pockets of sub-colonial
    darkness in rural backwaters;
The Virgin, too, is abducted by my warriors and bound to
    my desire;
Night and Silence have no power over my
Hard, undying light.

Separating Fire and Water

Naked women carry the candidate,
The Church of Food is burning;
The laughing Bacchus-mask
Wreathed in ivy
Floats in a milk of fog;
Driven by wires & clockwork it
Laughs through the centuries,
Past the millennium extravaganza
To a desiccated, sodden end, sea full of
Floating books, desert stacked with
Dry salted fish, sand blown through the
    hollow eye
Of the mind's ruins, the bleached,
    implacable skull
Of the truth.

Before the Convergence

Granted, we all have to pass again
Through whatever it was that killed us,
Transposed through the lookinglass right to left,
Enfolded in a wall of shimmering quicksilver,
To emerge where the Anti-Self lies in wait for us,
Extending a sly, left-handed handshake on the
Opposite shore of Death—

But, remember, Jose Arguelles,
There are two kinds of mirrors:
The dark smoking mirror of Tezcatlipoca
Where the soul is twisted till it becomes the mask,
And the crystal mask of Quetzalcoatl,
Holding not the face who is seen
But that other face—the one who watches.

The mirror masks and it unmasks,
It unveils and it disguises.
Wishing to hold himself something other
Than the face in the volcanic glass,
Quetzalcoatl on his raft of serpents was exiled
To the Western Paradise—

While the fool who thought he *was* the mask
Curled up like a snail shell
Fossilized in limestone
To become he hell inside the mirror.

Messiah

Who are we
Who were born at the end?
Are we the best, or the worst of men?
Latter-day saints,
Or demons in human form?
What bitter, medicinal juice
Was destined to be twisted out of us
That we came here to breathe, and walk
In this time
And at this place?

The warped mirror of this world
Caught your image, Messiah,
And nailed it to a blackened rock
Under a stream of barren, coursing thought.
That was the hook that dragged and lifted me
    from my sport
In the shining ocean of Beginning.

But now, as the air grows thin
And the bedrock wavers
You show yourself again
Through the fading veils
Of earth
And thought—
In the crypt of this secret chapel
Are milk and honey hid.

So lift dust and nugget, and pan them out.
Gold in the sack remembers the motherlode;
Honey in the pot remembers the mountain
    where it was born.
As sky sleeps, inverted, on the face of the
    ocean,
So now ocean rises, bodily,
And turns to sky entire.

Sacred Red and Blue Days

I

Bound
Under the sterile eyes of wolves;

Mothered to ash
In the ovens of time's end;

Born standing again
Under the new dispensation
On the paved earth —

Have we returned again to this battlefield
Only to recite the
Litany of our crimes?

Better to be
Featureless clay
In the hands of the Potter, fabricator
Of the Earth to come.

II

Knowledge is cash and cash is time
To sit in the concentric circles of your bloat
Hedged by psychic minefields,
The simple archaic alphabet of fear and desire....
Lesson One: you have escaped the consequences;
Lesson Two: the consequences are still there,
Fear looking inwards, toward the altar of Love,
Desire facing outwards, toward the altar of Fear....

My finger is on your shoulder,
Slight, constant pressure, easily bearable—
Except that I require that you simply turn

And face me now: Don't worry,
You have already been released;
I am only reading the record backwards,
As every death most certainly requires.

III

Whatever this contemporary river may be I must
   have missed it,
Having chosen for my "rendezvous with history"
Five years in a river of burning slag.
In that glowing bath, the chain that linked
   me to passing time
Melted completely away, except for these
   nuggets of ore
I am presently feeding
To that same burning river:
Fire fed to fire;
Chaos to chaos;
Repentance to sanctity;
Delusion to truth.

IV

Where were these hills, and where was I
When the thread was lost that bound us?
Is that why they now dream, heavy with sorrow
Locked in the cavern of the Earth-killer,
Where the footprint of the Secret Adam,
   the primordial Human Form, is rubbed out—
He of whom the Subtle Folk
Were the radiant elementals?
Is that why the buried skull of him is now filled
With the sniggering voices
Of the Jinn?

Only when man is Man again
Will these hills return from exile;
Only God's eye
Looking out through the eye of Man can see
    them as they are:
Gardens beneath which rivers flow,
Arteries of vitality and of truth.

V

If it is true that we will now fight all the old wars in reverse,
It is also true that, though loser now wins and winner loses,
The prize is not the same: death is life now, and life, death.

And the meanings of life and death, these too are reversed:
What we struggled all our lives for is simply what we were
    handed to begin with,
While the hand we were dealt by merciless fate, the very
    thing we fled from
Is perfected work now, image of the heart's desire.

VI

The struggle with the angel—it changes so fast.
He escaped through my grappling hands like
Snakes of quicksilver. Transmuted into lead,
I lived through the desert of his absence.
If I could fix the angel in stance, in breath,
In finest will, in subtlest practice, O my soul,
You know I would do it. I am nothing but the
Smoke of his gestures. God's is the light;
And his, the solid hand; and mine, the shadow.

VII

Stopped for interrogation at the apocalypse border,
All past history rolling in behind me, piling up
For the final burning—
All the treasures and the junk of karma,
Farewells that pierce the heart, then abandon it,
The vastness of endings,
The heavy weight of rotten fruit,
Huge decadence and fall.

We are the ones condemned to have a memory.
We stand and watch the death of the Sun
On an Aztec altar off the Farallones
Bleeding into the lap of Night....

Death is a completed planet in a distant sky,
   receding
Into the frigid bodiless blue of the Future
A whiff of liquid nitrogen, acrid and cold....
It's way past time for it, no question about it.
Whatever is capable of death
Was never capable of life, so let the
   purification proceed;
Let the fire grow fat on the
Dross in my soul;
Let death fall from me
Like a city.

VIII

That Word who left the mouth of God
To propagate himself in waves of Enlightenment
Comes back robed in his corpses, at cycle's end,
All the fates that tried to name him
Now the facets of a single crystal.
And, crossing the military border, his mirror-image,

The Serpent of Subtle Continuity, brother to the only
    Word God ever said
Between the gold and the lead
—He who establishes duration by the fixed
    burning-glass of present time—
Stands up. He wraps the risen Word around him
    in ascending spiral
Like an incandescent nerve,
Awakening him to One Form, One Man
Forged from myriad tiny unawakened beings
Curling to clotted dense sleep for
Fear of fire. All change joins
Tail to mouth around
The Jacob's Ladder,
The diamond axis
Of our dance.

IX

Your vision fills the waking world
Like the Sun. The Moon
(as Yeats said) will then be inside us,
"The Antithetical Tincture,"
The true aristocracy, where each man
(as Blake said) is "King & Priest
In his own house,"
Each of us a great Sun Door
In the solitude of his own soul—
Translucent crystal,
Window of fixed air—
Where the whole past is redeemed,
Returns effortlessly to the
Center of its own delight,
The empty mirror, the great expanse of
Conditionless space,
Prajñaparamita, she who is Space Herself when
Rung like a bell, clearing a path

For the Lightningbolt, the clapper that strikes
Between the root and the crown
Of anything.
His ministers shine out from the central
Void of his kingship
In twelve-thousand rays.

If he were brought into this world
With a heart and a face
He would be, precisely,
You yourself.

PART THREE:
A Metaphysical Exegesis
and Reader's Guide
to *The Wars of Love*

ONE

He who sings is a plucked string vibrating
Bound between two posts:
This perishing world
And the high walled garden of the King

Is the universe God? The answer is, Yes and No. Yes and No are the peak and trough of the sine wave of the primordial Tone: The *Shabd*; the *Naam*; the *Om*. The Logos is the first vibration, the Word begotten from all eternity, when turned toward cosmic manifestation; every created form both hides and expresses its own logos, the unique vibrational complex derived from the One and Only Spoken Word, the *kun!* of the Qur'an, the *fiat lux* of Genesis. *He who sings* is Adam, the Logos buried in the heart of Divinity, the Primordial Man. And Man, like a harpstring, does have two posts, two duties: To remember God and to face this world, where *all is perishing but His Face.*

Only That One knows his real name

Each created and living thing is a spoken Word of God—and whoever would speak must first listen: we are *sub*-creators, not co-creators: whatever we take into our hands to mold and shape has already been made before us, from the dawn of the first day.

And recalls it every day,

The universe is not established on its own foundation, but held in being by God's exquisitely instantaneous attention; in the words of the Noble Qur'an [55:29], *Each day He manifests himself in a new way.* "Recalls" is *speaks again*; is *remembers*; is *calls back.*

And in the canyons of the night
breathes him as he swims,
Fighting upstream to the source of his
hunger

Man's spiritual effort in traveling to God is already embraced by God's inbreathing and outbreathing of the Universe. We are exhaled into cosmic existence; we are inhaled into the Body of Life. Our desires for the things of this world are really His desire that there be a world in the first place; our desire to return to Him out of the wilderness of dimensional existence is really His desire to gaze upon Himself in the mirror of the human face.

> *A flashing salmon in the black river of*
> *dreams.*

For the heroic fish at the end of his life-cycle, *fana* becomes *baqa*. To attain the death which makes new life, the spawning salmon fights against the current of things-coming-into-existence, and so reaches the headwaters of the River of Life. This is my salute to the Celts, to poetry as a spiritual craft and to Lew Welch as my mentor in that craft, as well as to the Lewises and Moores and Duncans of my family tree who were my own tributaries, and the Norman/Cornish Uptons of Upton-upon-Severn. I, too, am Adam—I, too, am Man.

> *Searching earth and fire for your name,*
> *Beloved,*

—seeking, through vision and labor, through *jñana* and *karma,* through my second, Archetypal Parents who, as Plato told us in the *Timaeus,* are Solidity and Radiance, or Density and Light—

> *For your breast rising and falling in sleep*

—for the Sleeping God, Vishnu the Preserver, the Great Dreamer who dreams the universe.

> *He follows the wake of your Word*
> *On the face of your Ocean—*
> *She whose waves*
> *Have never stopped moving him*
> *In the paths of this house of dust.*

His Ocean is His Essence, in which all existence is drowned. The waves are the spacio-temporal existents, who are without self-existence, who have no essence or existence but His. Seeking God, all things follow His waves, His signs. Yet the wave has no essence but the water. Each one who seeks Him seeks across the face of Him, within the very Essence of Him. As long as they think He is elsewhere, they never find Him. Seeking water across the face of all the seas, their inheritance is a handful of dust—the destiny of all forms—that sand upon which no house can be built. The world, to them, is a world of facts—of things already "made" and therefore already dying—of the reign of quantity—of the statistical mass. But when the wind of creation drops, when the waves of existence stop rolling, then behind the face of He, the Radiant Creator, reclines the formless form of She, the Black Essence.

> Never. You never came into existence. You stayed wound in self-ken,
> lapped in Your own delight.

And the signature of the unknowable Divine Essence is: "Before creation (said Muhammad), God was alone, One without a second, companionless." "And (said Ali) He is even now as He was."

> Ships were sent out from Your harbor at midnight, but never found
> You.

That which is Its own self-knowledge cannot find Itself beyond Itself because there is no such thing as "beyond Itself." God's refusal to manifest Himself is the beginning of His Self-manifestation; the Kabbalists call it *Tsim-Tsum*, the merciful withdrawal of the Deity into His own Secret Essence to "make room" for the universe.

> There was no breach in Your courtesy; no guest was turned back from
> your door.
> Only I, of all your companions, was sent away empty.
> I adopted your own method then. I shared your impassiveness. I was
> as annihilated in the heart of You
> As You had ever been.

All potential existences were content to rest in God—except the one that said: "For me to claim to be God is to be other than God. Then let me claim the tiny cosmic existence God has given me, so that I might, in that emptiness, let God alone be God. Only in the poverty of my own noth-ingness before the face of God, can God be God indeed"; in the words of al-Hallaj, "To assert that God is One is thereby to set up another beside Him". That first Human Form, that first reflexive face of God within God, knew that the only way that he, as God's first step of departure from God, could attain to God, was to be annihilated in Beyond Being— an annihilation that al-Hallaj enacted in the flesh. God is the Coy Beloved who plays hard to get—but two can play at that game.

> I heard your suitors singing and pleading in the alley behind your
>   balcony;
> I heard the heedless drunkards
> Pounding at your door.

Creation has begun. The permanent archetypes have begun to seek their Essence. The desire to return to God has initiated the cosmic journey away from God, all within the Essence of God.

> So when first dawn broke over the waiting sea, the black dividing-line
>   of the horizon
> Left us in peace, careful not to remind us
> Of something we might forget
> If our vigilance ever faltered, distracted for a moment
> By the cry of a bird.

God loses nothing by creating the Universe; He is even now as He was. The archetypes of all things, the "generations in the loins of Adam", are not disturbed by the first stirrings of their outer manifestation. They remain profoundly at rest. And yet the possibility of forgetfulness has now been born, within the steady, intrinsic vigilance of those who have never, can never, and will never forget.

> Then the cry broke. The image of the rising sun in the world ocean
> Shattered into a million sparks, under a seething wind,
> Till every spoken word declared its separate existence,
> Remembering quite clearly how it had been spoken by You,
> Whose silence was never kept, and never broken.

No-one left You when the world was made. None were excluded, none
   arrived.
Your hospitality was perfect.

The Breath of the Merciful, *al-Nafas al-Rahman*, confers real existence
upon the *ayan al-thabita*, the permanent archetypes, hovering in virtual
existence. God says, *Am I not your Lord?* and all of them answer *Yea!*
God loses nothing by liberating the archetypes into formal existence.
What happened when that happened never happened, what happened
when that happened was never prevented; these are God's Generosity
and His Jealousy, the two faces of His Mercy. There is no difference
between them. He is even now as He was; the "ten-thousand things" are
even now as they were within Him.

I am Your secret; You are mine. We never told it.

Primordial Adam is God's eternal self-knowledge; God is Adam's
Essence. My secret Essence is God, the *atman*; "My truest 'I' is God'",
Meister Eckhart says. And the secret essence of God is Man, who is
God's eternal Self-knowledge within the Secret of His own nature,
called by the Muslims *al-Insan al Kamil*, personified by them as Muham-
mad, and by the Christians the Second Person of the Blessed Trinity, the
Lamb begotten—and slain—before the foundation of the world. And a
secret told is no longer secret, therefore no longer tellable—and so the
Secret remains.

   The long ages waited and suffered to learn that secret
   —cry of the Eagle never given above the listening sea—
   Only to discover that they themselves were the secret,

Time is Adam's sequential deployment. But time cannot survey itself,
any more than space can encompass itself. Creation cannot encompass
the Creator, nor manifestation embrace the Unmanifest, no matter how
long it waits or struggles. Yet the Unknowable is the principle by which
all things are known, and that Principle is eternally within us. When "I
want to know That" dies, it gives birth to "That art Thou!"

And that You alone were privy
To the script buried in the breath, rising and falling through the
    checkerboard of nights and days,
Opening Your eyes, and then closing them, on the kingdom of sleep
Where the roar of Your risen hand silences time,
And the perfume of Your name
Brings news from the Garden.

Only God is Witness to time and history, to the seasons of the year, to
the pulsations of the artery. The passing instants, the passing years, the
passing *manvantaras* are His breath: the Days and Nights of Brahman. In
eternity, God knows all things as Himself; in time, He knows them as
Himself with eyes open, and as not-Himself with eyes closed—these
being the creation and destruction of the universe, aeon by aeon, instant
by instant. The impermanence of phenomena in time is their emptiness
in eternity; the emptiness of phenomena in eternity is their lack of any
essence but His.

I am your Face within you. You gazed on that Face, before the beginning,
    without me.

Primordial Adam is God's eternal Self-knowledge, but the Self-knowl-
edge of the One does not compromise the Unity of the One; in God
there is no-one "else"; in Him, to know is not other than to be.

I was the widening echo of Your name
Over the virgin waters, when you knew yourself One Form, human
    and more-than-human,

The face of the Primordial Adam turned toward creation is Metatron,
Adam Kadmon, *al-Insan al-Kamil*, the theophany of God as Person
within human consciousness, the quintessential manifestation and syn-
thetic epitome of the formal or Essential Pole, which emanates the Spiri-
tual or Metacosmic Sun—

Blazing like the Sun with archangelic rays, the ranked fountains of Power
    incandescent with knowledge of You, pouring motionless from your
    burning Core

—that Sun which is Transcendent Intellect as creative Logos, the Primordial Adam speaking all the Names God taught him, radiating them as the realm of the Living Archetypes, the Archangelic domain, *al-Jabarut*, which in turn emanates *al-Malakut*—

> Then shooting up all around You, trees whose limbs are conscious aeons
> and living numbers, eternal fixed dimensions and histories cut in
> crystal,

—the Angelic domain, the higher intermediary plane, which in turn emanates the lower intermediary plane that accepts the subtle impressions of all physical realities in their hour of death, as well as imprints from the Angelic Plane per se —

> Whose branches are the swift messengers, signatures of fire, pages of
> the shifting rock-face breathing and moving,

—the lower intermediary plane being the realm of subtle nature, the Kingdom of the Jinn, which in turn emanates—

> Whose blossoms are galaxies and starclusters, the herds of deep ocean
> gliding like mountains, bird-nations exploding from the lake in a
> storm of their own language,

the material domain, *al-Mulk*, under which is hidden the Substantial Pole—

> Thunder of bison across the plains
> Of Your ancient and open hand,

—the *prima materia*, the realm of Yin, that Formless receptivity which underlies and supports all form, the invisible Motherhood of God. The Lakota call Her Grandmother Earth—she whose first daughter is the *materia secunda*, Mother Earth, whose symbolic beast is the Buffalo. And the secret of the Buffalo, is that all we see when we look to South, into this created world, is the Buffalo unfolded into all the places and times, all the forms and events of the universe. But where the Buffalo really

[110]

lives is in the North—behind our eyes, not in front of them—and in the North, the Buffalo is all forms and events, all places and times at once. In Blake's mythology, this is the seat of the Zoa Urthona, the "Earth Owner".

> All humbling themselves to know You,
> Offering breath and meat and name as sacrifice to their Creator,

When *al-Insan al-Kamil* was first deployed as *al-Jabarut*, the Realm of Power, he was sacrificed—like Purusha, like Ymir—dismembered to create all things; in order to realize and reconstitute him, to attain to the Paradise of the Creator, the Divine Throne, all things must sacrifice themselves in return, so as to rise to their archetypes as embraced by the Logos, which holds and reveals all the archetypal Forms and Revelations by which, according to God's will, Man is to subsist on Earth.

> To be the seeds of tongues and laws, rites and doctrines,
> Bricks in the walls of the human city,
> Where the secret names of all things,
> The stars standing in wait from the beginning
> Pour themselves, willingly,
> Red blood leaping from severed arteries,
> Into the crucible of the Human Form.

And the cosmic fruit of this sacrifice is the Incarnate Human Form, whose *Shakti* is spiritual human culture based upon Divine Revelation both *to* Man and *through* him. The elements, the minerals, the plants, the animals, the planets, the galaxies are composed of a limited number of God's Names; the Human Form is composed of *all* of them—which is why all things, in recognizing that Form, make sacrifice to it, seeking their own fullness of being in what is ontologically above them, reaching their apotheosis in the consciousness of Man. Blake: "The gods should sacrifice to Man, not Man to the gods".

> See now the making of a Man! Watch, in this man-making, how the
>   universe itself is unfolded
> From the secret place.

The Human Form, as the epitome of cosmic manifestation, is created in the same way that the universe is; the universe, as the full deployment of the Human Form, is created in the same way that the Human Form is. But the creation of Man, unlike that of the universe, encompasses and manifests both *al-Rahman* and *al-Rahim*, both the path of Creation and the path of Return. It is by this that Man transcends the universe; it is by this that God commanded that the angels prostrate to Adam, because Adam alone knew the names of all things, including the names of the angels themselves, since he was composed of them.

> Your mother is purest water
> In the womb of My being; My Spirit moves on the face of her
> To write the Name of Unity
> On the white scroll of your heart.

The Mother of Man is Holy Wisdom. She is the Guarded Tablet, unlettered like the Prophet Muhammad, empty of words, images and pre-conceptions, Virgin to the Sublime Pen of the Holy Word, the listening darkness within Muhammad that heard the word 'Recite!' (She is white in this world, black in that; black by the dazzling superabundance of the light of the Essence.) Her earthly form was Mary; her celestial form was and is Mary, Queen of Heaven. When we "become pure prayer", when our Heart becomes Virgin, she awakens within us, within the darkness of our natural being, as the Superessential Darkness of the Divine Essence, as That which is purely and only Itself, and—simultaneously—totally Beyond Itself. In this world, she is a pure white scroll standing ready for the Name and the Law; in that world, She is the darkness of Beyond Being that allows God to be born—which is why it is said in Kabbalah that the words of Torah are written in an ink of white fire, upon a scroll of black fire.

> And the fish of every sea
> Will rise to that bait,
> Because you are the gathered hunger of all things
> To suffer human form, and employ human speech
> Only to pronounce that single Name: Allah—
> Word of their origin
> Gone home in fire.

To Him, to Allah, *is the return of all things*—but only through Man. It is by this that Man is *khalifa*; it is by this that he assumed the Trust. When man, the epitome of all created things, who is also the quintessential *experience* of all creatures, pronounces the name *Allah* in the midst of the cosmic conditions in which he is immersed, he leads all things back to God in that instant. They have no other road.

Can eternity deepen? Can God become more God than yesterday?
Where there is no tomorrow, how can the sleepless Eye awaken from
    its sleep?
And what wall can stand unshaken in that House
Where rock is wind and light is sliced in planes like a diamond
To stop eternity from deepening on the End of all things
Who rests without end?

If Eternity were "fixed" it would be dead. "Do not call it fixity" said Eliot in the *Four Quartets*; rather, he said, we should name it "the still point of the turning world". On the other hand, if Eternity were capable of passing, like time does, it would not be Eternity. If, as Plato says in the *Timaeus*, "Time is the moving image of Eternity", then Eternity is equally the "static" pattern of motion itself, vibrating around its own inviolable Center like a "standing wave", changing without passing, revealing ever-new faces of Itself in every eternal instant while in no way negating or obscuring its "earlier" faces, and doing so with neither "growth" nor "increase" nor "improvement" nor "evolution"—since if God, the Principle of the Eternal, is not yet God, not yet Absolute, Infinite and Perfect, then He never will be. (Mock on, mock on, Teilhard de Chardin, and Sri Aurobindo, and Rudolph Steiner, and Alfred North Whitehead.) God, to Himself, can be neither a disconcerting surprise nor a foregone conclusion. He is never startled; He is never bored. Yet Gregory Palamas speaks of "progress" in Eternity—not the progress of God, but the ever-deepening understanding and love of God on the part of the blessed. And in a way—since Man is the principle of God's Self-knowledge—this is also an eternal deepening of God's understanding and love of Himself. Yet this "deepening", being eternal, is never not present. "I am Jehovah", He says; "I have not changed." But He also says, "Behold, I make all things new". *Because* He has not changed, He makes all things new. *Because* He has never been so much as brushed by

the tip of the final feather of the wing of the flying bird of change—
change which is nothing but an endless dying—He *is* the renewal of all
things: *All is perishing, except His face.*

> Love cannot grow and must grow. My knowledge of You must fight
> to the Heart of You
> Till You obey my command and cry my name and make me real to
> know You.

On the path of Love, nothing separates lover and Beloved but the lover's
love for that very Beloved. 'I want to eat sugar, not become sugar' Sri
Ramakrishna said. And on the path of Knowledge, nothing separates the
knower from the Thing Known but knower's knowledge of that very
Object. We can never love Love Itself unless we *become* Love; we can
never know Knowledge Itself until we *become* Knowledge. But we (the
small, the contingent, the servant) can never become That (the Vast, the
Self-Sufficient, the Lord); this is precisely why Annihilation must super-
vene, and settle the matter. *We* cannot call God's Name; who are we to
name the Nameless, the Absolute? But God *can* call *our* name; this is one
thing that Annihilation and *ishk*—self-annihilating spiritual passion—
have within their power. God, the Nameless, calls His own Name, and
that Name is *I*; only then can I call my own Name, annihilating all self-
reference and self-definition within It, and have that Name be He.

> I want to shake my living name from Your lips—but Your knowledge
> of me is finished already, and mine of You—only endless.
> The carven smile by which You know and accept
>
> all that I am,
>
> Before I speak or breathe or
>
> lift my hand
>
> Drives me from Your door.
>
> I want the sweetness of love, and
> the bitterness of it:
> I want the trophies of War.

Because when I asked You
How perfect love could grow and perfect knowledge deepen, Your
answer was:

Through absence

The servant can never be the Lord, therefore he can never love Him as
He deserves to be loved or know Him as He deserves to be known. But
he *does* love Him, he *does* possess knowledge of Him—imperfect love,
incomplete knowledge—and so he must leave Him. Eternity, under the
power of exclusive Transcendence, has become the fixed, the finished,
the dead; consequently Immanence must now be sought in the wilder-
ness of time, duality, and conflict. If Eternity appears to be without
Mercy, then time must become that Mercy—a hard Mercy, in the face of
which the only true Mercy is Eternity.

Your knowledge of Your Black Essence is deepening in Your own
Eternity without motion or passage,

Layla!

And this is Your withdrawal from us, the momentary distracted
glance
That burst a cosmos of stars through the eye of a needle, and sent
them on their journey, across an ever-widening distance,
The light of them reddening, bleeding, like memory itself,
To the final borders of space and time....
The Universe is the autumn of God, embroidered curtain
Closed on the balcony....

And just as Eternity's freedom from change has become the vision of
stony aloofness and petrification, so Eternity's freedom from that very
petrification has become the vision of time as an endless departure and
dissipation and loss of God—a dissipation that began at the Big Bang,
and is now manifesting as the redshift of the expanding, dying
universe—as if the stars themselves were reddening as they leave us, in a
kind of autumnal nostalgia, as they sweep us ever further from the radi-
ant face of God. "The whole universe is on fire" said the Buddha;
"Memory is Eternal Death" said William Blake.

and when You, Who demanded nothing,
    bowed to my demand
That You send me away to suffer and die and win
The proofs of love,
I felt only Your rejection;
(When we complain of Your decrees
The memory of that first generosity
Puts us all to shame.)

When, in pre-eternity, He asked us *Am I not your Lord?*, and we answered
Him *Yea!*—thus establishing the primordial and world-creating polarity
between Lord and Servant—He unleashed matter, energy, space and
time, He burst the galaxies into existence; at the same time He withdrew,
in *tsim-tsum,* to "make room" for them. But what we see only as His
rejection, is in reality His merciful discretion. We asked to be born, after
all—and so, in perfect compliance with our wish, he veiled His burning
and annihilating Face.

Then You threw me into a magic sleep, and cut me open,
And drew the world from my side,
Radiant, veiled as a bride, in all the beauty of Your Names;
But I could not meet her price. The seething ocean
Took her image.

God can create a universe without departing from Himself or losing
Himself; not so when it comes to Man. (Beware, O poet!) Though it was
God Himself who created Eve from the rib (or *liver*) of Adam, when
Adam first looked upon her, he saw a helpmeet, an Other. Here is where
creation itself, though it is in no way a Fall but rather a radiant manifesta-
tion of its Principle, is in another way the beginning of the Fall, since
differentiated existence (in the Object, in Eve) is inseparable from differ-
entiable *choice* (in the Subject, in Adam)—and where choice exists,
wrong choice becomes possible; thus Adam's disobedience was, in one
way, a fruit of God's command-to-obedience itself. From the standpoint
of free will—which can never be denied—Adam knew what was right,
and chose what was wrong, and was entirely free to do so; thus the true
guilt of Original Sin. But from the standpoint of emanation and All-

Possibility—which can never be denied—somewhere, somehow, that wrong choice was destined to be made—thus the *felix culpa*, and the precedence of Redemption over Creation. Nonetheless the Fall, though inevitable, and a lawful and necessary part of Providence and the Divine economy, was terribly real. "There needs be evil", said Jesus, "but woe to him through whom evil comes". And so Eve, though she was inseparable from Adam in Eternity, was lost to him through sin, through the dizzying descent from spiritual, unitary, cardiac knowledge—*Intellectus*—to divided, discursive, cerebral knowledge—*ratio*—which shattered the vision of Eve, dis-membered her and buried the fragments within the "ten-thousand things". Once his soul, his beloved, she was now merely his world, his "environment".

And the covenant we made was this: That the day I remembered her,
And spoke her name,
And gathered her from the face of all things—
She who left at dawn to become my world, came home at twilight to
    be my soul—
You would also remember me,
And acknowledge my struggle,
Standing at Your threshold,
Victorious and wounded,
Obedient to Your command.

As soon as the Fall is complete, the path of Return also dawns in its completeness; this is why Adam, the first transgressor, was also the first prophet. There are steps to it. To gather Eve together from the face of all things is to complete the lesser, feminine mysteries, to accomplish psychic recollection, and thereby to re-establish the integral, primordial, Adamic Human Form. But hidden within the lesser mysteries are also the greater—because when the withdrawal of the unconscious projection of psychic contents upon the things, persons and situations of the outer world is completed—thus leading to the attainment of "know thyself" on the psychic level—the world itself dissolves. It is transformed from a fragmentary collection of discrete objects into a unitary field of sentient Energy, into *Shakti*. And when *Shakti* dawns, this means that the *imago dei* within us, the Absolute Witness, the *atman* has been unveiled; this is the attainment of "know thyself" on the pneumatic level.

When we overcome our psychic dismemberment, when we are re-membered, then God remembers us—or rather, we come into the field of God's eternal remembering of us. And when God remembers us, we become capable of remembering Him; his Name appears within us; this is when "the day star shall arise in your hearts" [Peter 1:19]. And when this mutual remembering is firmly established, such that there is no longer a hair's-breadth of distinction between the Remember and the Remembered, then the spiritual path is complete.

But for this to happen, the Fall must first be completed; Man must feel the hard, unyielding, but nonetheless balancing and stabilizing, ground beneath his feet. He must fall so far that he becomes, for good or ill— either as abased by his puny pride or as exalted by his mighty humility— his own sorry self alone. That man could finally be *individual* man, the only Path back from *kosmos* to Deity (as no community can be saved *as* community, as no church congregation or monastic brotherhood ever became a saint), that his exile might reach its furthest point, and thus its end, the Spartans died at Thermopylae. In doing so they liberated—for both good and ill—the Individual from the archaic theocratic civiliza-tions. (In earlier world-ages, human individuality was not simply immersed in a *participation mystique*; it was simultaneously more per-fectly embedded in its spiritual and natural and social environments, and more perfectly self-realized and free from the bonds of those environ-ments, than we men of Kali-yuga can easily imagine; we can perhaps see a true remnant of this condition in the world of the Lakota. But in the Old World, by the time the Greeks fought the Persians, this was no longer the case.) And Homer knew it already. All of Odysseus' men, all of Penelope's one-hundred and eight suitors, eventually had to be killed off—all those projections withdrawn—all those fragments recollected. Past the number one-hundred and eight, which, as the number of the Golden Mean, is the symbol of *kosmos* and manifestation, only the Alone can make flight to the Alone.

TWO

When God looked down at the Earth He had just then made,
It opened, like an eye.

"The Eye through which I see God," said Meister Eckhart, "and the Eye
through which He sees me, are the same Eye." God does not only wit-
ness the Earth; He also witnesses the vision of His universal manifesta-
tion *through* the Earth. If He did not also look through her, the Earth
would be dead, because she would not be necessary.

Adam and Eve stood that day
On a ground without memory—an Earth which did not contain
within it
The bones of the human dead.

When we are completely awake, when we fully and consciously live our
experience, leaving no karmic residues, then there is no such thing as
memory, no such thing as time. There is no "collective unconscious"; no
smoke of incomplete experience darkens the air; no dead husks of the
past—generated, withered, and cast off in sleep, like the cocoons of
insects, like the *klipoth*—litter the ground, or sink below it to form the
realm of Hades, where "memory is Eternal Death". In the beginning,
Eternity is not heavenly, in the sense of distant and abstract, but earthly,
in the sense of concrete and present: God "walks with Man in the cool of
the evening."

Adam was a word of God, striding through Eden;
In Eve God lay, and listened. Inside his heart Adam saw
The names of the Creator engraved on the guarded tablet;
Before his eye in the body of Eve he saw the shapes of his children,
struggling to be born, and named them out—fish and animals and
birds, mountains and stars—into the cold outer air.

These are the Yang and Yin, the vertical dimension that unites manifes-
tation with Source, and the horizontal dimension that deploys manifesta-
tion, purifies it, and makes it receptive to Source. In Islamic esoterism,
the Guarded Tablet is the Yin power, symbolized by the Arabic letter *ba*;

it is vertical as the hierarchy of universal manifestation, the Great Chain of Being, and horizontal as the receptivity of universal manifestation to God's Word. In this mode it is the receptive "page" upon which the purely vertical Yang power, symbolized by the letter *Alif*, the Divine Pen, God's creative Act descending vertically out of the Unknowable, writes the words of all things—or, from another perspective, *uncovers* the words of all things. According to Q: 21:30–33, Adam, by God's command, told the angels their Names; he could do so because he, as *al-Insan al-Kamil*, the Perfect Man, was the cosmic and metacosmic epitome of God's Self-revelation, the synthesis of all His Names. He knew those Names because he was composed of them. This is why he was able to name the animals in Eden [Genesis 2:20]—because he recognized them as the cosmic reflections of the angels, the conscious, individualized forms of the Names of God.

From that day, Adam and Eve walked on the earth as human gods,

"I have said 'Ye are Gods'" [Psalm 82; quoted by Jesus in John 10:34]

Through a world they carved together out of Space with the
crossed rays of their vision.

A living world of manifestation must be composed of the bi-unity of Transcendence and Immanence. Transcendence alone ends in the dissolution of all form; Immanence alone ends in the abstract wilderness of dead matter—which comes to the same thing. When Transcendence and Immanence are divorced in a given world, that world ends.

All things were mirrors to them: the lichen-studded rocks and bones
of their ancestors,
Shaggy tree-lords and the dark herds of ocean,

If you know yourself as existing not by your own self-concept, but only as witnessed by God, then God is mirrored back to you in all the forms of the world. It is by this that the world you live in lives. But if you fall under the power of your self-concept and begin to worship it, your world will mirror back to you only that alienated self-concept, and thus become alien to you—lost.

[120]

The magnetic cyclone of the frigate-birds above a sunken world,

This is Atlantis—according to the legend that seabirds circling above the waves of the Atlantic Ocean are trying to return to their former home in that sunken continent. Here Adam and Eve appear as the father and mother of this present cycle of humanity, Atlantis representing the previous one.

Roots of volcanoes echoing the thunder of the stars,

The power stored within nature, the *potentia* of it, is the *kundalini*—the Celestial Light hidden within the darkness of matter; if the creative Logos were not within matter as well above it, there could be no world. In the words of the Noble Qur'an, *God is the Light of the heavens and the earth.*

The animal faces of their own organs and kingdoms under the Eagle's
    gaze—

The animals are the outer reflections of the names of God of which the Human Form is composed; the Eagle is immanent Intellection.

And the shapes of their own names—Adam and Eve, herm and
    dolmen—
Stalking the forests of each other's vision. Where their two visions
    crossed
Was Eden. Where they forked
Was dark self-love.

The separation of Transcendence and Immanence is the beginning of the Fall.

The widening circles of God's creative Wind
Crossing the ocean of cosmos, the face of the mirror,
Shattered the disk of the Sun into rippling snakes
And seeded the dream-universe.
A ghost of Eve took shape in Adam's eye;

A memory of Adam stood hard in the eye of Eve,
The Beasts of the Four Quarters.
That's when we all began to dream each other,

The Spirit or Breath or Wind of God moving upon the face of the waters
in Genesis may be seen as that which breaks up the unitary image of God
in the receptive depths of *maya-in-divinis*, the Divine Feminine within
Him, and by so doing creates the universe. And inseparable from this
creation is the self-reflexiveness of the innumerable sentient beings of
which the universe is composed. When multiplicity is born, egoic sub-
jectivity is born—consequently our subjective images of each other
begin to replace the true vision of each other as mirrors of God, empty
of separate self-nature.

Till our children became like a swarm of bees in the green shadows of
    the pool,
Field of warm, buzzing energy on the borders of sleep.

Here *reproduction* begins on the subtle plane. To exist as subjective visions
of ourselves and each other is to fail of perfect Being, a failure that makes
it necessary for us to keep "trying again", this being the archetypal source
of biological reproduction on the subtle plane, and the reason for it—as
well as the source of and reason for time itself. The "field of warm buzz-
ing energy" is Etheric Plane, the realm of subtle material forces, where
the prototypes of material creation are shaped by the intelligible forms of
the higher archetypal worlds, and prepared for outer manifestation.

Eve dreamt that she wandered East, toward the Gates of Birth,
Till she reached Eden's boundary. All beyond that gunmetal-blue
    line
Was grey, shifting ocean. She heard the Sea-beast call her name.

"Mother!" she cried. "When did I lose you? How could I have
    forgotten you? I can't remember—
It was on a beach somewhere; I remember now; I fell asleep in the
    sand and dreamt you were a whale;
You sank below me, miles down; I cried; I couldn't find you."

As soon as Eve ceases to be the *human* form of the Earth, the Earth appears as something outside her, a material object *previous* to her which is also the *source* of her—something awesome, elemental, and inaccessible—a Lost Mother, lost as soon as posited: the Chaos Archon.

> (And while she lay, weeping and demanding, on the shores of non-
> entity,
> The Land-beast rose inside her, occupying the stations of her spine,
> the desert strongholds,
> Red flickering torches on a moonless night....)

To see an external material object as one's origin leads one to conceive, in rebellion against this terrifying alienation, the sense of one's isolated, individual, Promethean self-will as one's origin—which, of course, is only a further alienation. And so a second Archon, the Archon of Self-hood, is born.

> Adam, in a separate dream, bit into an apple, and tasted blood.
> He called Eve's name. The cry rose above him, his words like iron
> birds.
> They solidified into the ashen face and frozen beard of the Alien God,
> hooded eagle on his wrist, tongues of flame licking the empty
> sockets.

> Adam stumbled in his dream. His shield was broken.
> He crept westward toward the Gates of Death—
> And the outer darkness poured in upon him,
> Beat against his named and defended image like a torrent of birds,
> All grasping claws and stabbing beaks.
> He was beaten to his knees, and so lifted his eyes to his father
> Memory, the Alien God.
> A crushing weight of stone, carved with the fixed runes of history
> Settled on the crown of his skull.

Adam begins to sense the fall of Eve, her alienation from him—an alienation which is due to her identification with (in other words, her alienation from) an external material nature, an Earth Mother. Every ego-identification with a thing is, ironically, an alienation from that thing;

identification can seek the One only by first positing the Two. To the degree that Eve has fallen from the Human Form to the level of an Earth Mother, she has become, to Adam, not a women, but a breast—a breast that immediately loses even its mammal warmth, and becomes a cold, crisp apple instead. And as soon as Adam bites into the forbidden fruit of elemental Nature, he himself loses the Human Form; the God that had been the Divine Witness within him becomes an external, distant, merciless divine tyrant instead—a third Archon, the Archon of Law. His loss of the Human Form, his fall into elemental Nature, into a perpetual generation that is inseparable from endless death, makes him totally vulnerable to the subhuman forces of that Nature, including automatic, unconscious, sub-vocal thought: the attacking birds. And his vulnerability to the powers of sub-human, elemental Nature forces him to turn even further toward the abstract idea of Transcendence as refuge from them. But abstract Transcendence is not truly Transcendent; it is nothing but the dead memory of past instances of the breakthrough of Eternity into Time, frozen into alienated religious legend with no *understanding* behind it, petrified into a blind mechanistic Law that allows for no understanding of the *telos* of Law, of the eternal Truths that any sacred Law is designed to transmit. The purpose of sacred law is to pacify and empower the will, in the name of the Divine Intellect in Man, so as to prepare the human will to submit to, and consequently function as an *existential understanding* of, the eternal Truths the Divine Intellect reveals.

> Then he rose from death in Eden, and
> walked East through the shadow of death, in a pouring dream,
> toward the arms of his beloved,
> Head still spinning from the stroke of the double axe.

Suffering under this terrible loss of the Human Form, Adam tries to embrace fallen Nature as his lost human soul—but until the Fall is complete, and (much, much later) until God establishes for man the Way of Return by the words of His Prophets, this can never be. For the Sufis, the double axe symbolizes "detachment from this world, detachment from the next." Here, however, it appears in ironic mode as "*loss* of this world, *loss* of the next." The double axe was originally an archaic Minoan symbol of the waxing and waning phases of the Moon—crescent and decrescent—and thus (in this context) of the sub-lunary world, where the cycles of nature replace the vision of the Eternal Present.

(The crack of the hunter's rifle called up blackbirds in a cloud;
Their song, like a turning wheel.)

Redwing blackbirds. The hunter hunts the Names of God, to kill and eat and make an identity for himself *inside* himself, apart from God; the paleolithic hunter now spends half his time in Plato's Cave—his psyche—surrounded not by animals but by their depicted images painted on the cave's walls. So now time, that once was an eternal vibration, begins to become a circle, revolving around a distant, abstract, conjectural Center, but unable to rest in it—a Center symbolized by, though not really incarnated as, the Pole Star.

Eve looked up. She rose, in her dream, from the face of the waters,
And called Adam home to her out of the bloody, dying West—
But what rose to that call, and advanced to meet her, like a walking
    tower, a moving cliff, a tree burnt out by lightning
Was not a man, nor did it have the smell of a man.
She called her beloved's name and started a black crag walking.
It stood before her; impenetrable, aloof.
She touched it, caressed it; she wept to make it animal, make it
    human:
Cold unresponsive stone
Cast back her echo.

Adam has now become a heartless stone of sacrifice. He has lost the Human Form. When Man can no longer see God in Nature, Nature can no longer see God in Man. The orgiastic women, weeping for Tammuz, are weeping for their own loss. What had been the adamantine Spirit within the human Heart is now nothing but a pretty adolescent boy, gored by a boar, castrated, buried with formal lamentations, to touch the sweetly vicious soul of Eve now degraded to the state of material nature, whose greatest delight is to mourn orgiastically—to say: "I am Death, my child, my poor murdered lover, and Death can never die"—whereas the truth is, in the words of William Blake, that "Memory is Eternal Death"—the dismembered perpetually remembered, over and over again, in a trance of lethal nostalgia. Here Eve tries to summon Adam as the Human Form to return to her and save her, but she is able to invoke only the Selfhood Archon into which Adam has fallen.

> Then she died against the face of it, over and over again, in the
>   autumn of every year
> To become the flesh of the crabbed and shrunken
> World we know.

Either Eve, as the Great Mother, the Archon of Chaos, must sacrifice Adam as the young dying-and-resurrected god, or else Adam, as the God of the Underworld, as Hades the chthonic Archon of Selfhood, must sacrifice Eve as Chaos' innocent and unprotected daughter, the raped and abducted Maiden—Persephone. The soul of Eve cannot remain free from the cycles of fallen time and nature, even as Eternal Death. She thought she could (at least) act as the Matrix where Adam, now shrunk to Attis or Adonis, would turn through death and rebirth *inside* her forever; but she herself ultimately becomes swept up in that endless death-and-rebirth; she is not immune to it. Goddess though she be, she cannot retain the Human Form, even as a memory. The human soul, exiled from Eternity, dispersed in the elements, becomes the "vain repetition" spoken of by Augustine in *City of God*, the endless cycles of the natural world. The Earth longs to return to her original home in the Human Form, but can find no access, no way back.

William Blake, in the Introduction to the *Songs of Experience*, "The Voice of the Bard", speaks as Adam calling to the lost Eve: "O Earth O Earth return!.... Why wilt thou turn away [i.e., why do you continue to turn in your vain repetition?]/ The starry floor/ The watry shore/ Is giv'n thee till the break of day."

> I have laid the foundation of my house, said Adam,
> On a sand the Book says is the devil's sand.
> My premises move and slide under my feet.
> I have planted my seed in a plot where the furrows shift,
> Raking the sprouting stems left and right....

This cavern or grotto, shouldered by the green tide,
Echoes with the moaning of whales, the herds of ocean rippling like
    wheat,
Fish speaking in the click of rock,
Language hammering the dumb shore.
My story, my mirror's cherished profile—him I'd leave behind
    gladly, in a casket of words—
He has found neither home nor work.
He wanders from field to field of abstract merchandise, visions sown
    in him against his will,
Reaped without his knowledge.
He drowns, or I drown;
He drowns in me, or I in his flotsam, his carrion;
We go down struggling like brothers into deep Ocean... groans of fish
    bleeding from cut bellies....
Their diamond skulls, sunken treasure, roll down the submarine cliff
Into a deeper grave, or origin-pit,
Wrapped in a deeper word.
Not glowing skulls but shining babies dream there,
Give throat-birth to their spoken words
Like silver fish. And I—(Fool!)—I listen
To every one of them. My language is infused, infested
With the begged-for broken detritus of birth and death,
The black tetragrammaton, the four nucleic acids,
Of babies slaughtered for bardic power.
Cattle, Bison, Deer, Pig, Antelope,
Five species, five languages,
Bound through an atmosphere of water;
Heaving the shoulder of their silent Wave against me;
Drinking my breath.

The petrification of the human form as Selfhood, as isolated individual-
ity, invokes the counter-Archon, who is Chaos, the dissolution of form.
They are inseparable—just as Adam, as the second Archon, the Archon
of Selfhood, is bound to that very Selfhood as if it were another being,
twinned with it. "'I' is another" said Arthur Rimbaud—by which he
might have meant "My truest 'I' is God" (Eckhart)—but judging from

that Leviathan of his, rotting in those phosphorescent, infernal marshes, he was more likely referring to *the ego as parasite*, the archonic counterfeit of the Atman, that great Myself without whom I cannot live, and who lives by devouring me from within. And human speech, once the fully conscious rendering of the eternal archetypes, is reduced—in the "collective unconscious" that James Joyce spoke for in *Finnegan's Wake*—to the automatic, the elemental, the embryonic. Adam, by the verbal sorcery initiated by the Fall, tries to re-establish the Unfallen World; of course he fails. Who recognizes himself as a Word of God can speak his own words; who loses this recognition becomes host to the hungry parasite of human language. His words do his speaking for him. His tongue splits in two, like a serpent's tongue. And all the kings horses and all the kings men, and all the poetry and the magic of the spoken word, and even the very human sacrifice it ultimately leads to, cannot reconstitute the Primordial Adam now fallen and dispersed in the elements; they only shatter and dismember him further. Each word, like a piranha or a barracuda or a moray eel, like Scylla the sea-monster, takes a different piece of him. The Words of God were Adam's members—animals in this world [Genesis 2:20], angels in that other [Q. 21:30–33]. But now, under the delusion of the Fall, he believes that they are *his* words, not God's. The poet arrogates to himself God's sovereign power to speak words of truth of his own contrivance; consequently he becomes the one who *says what he does not* [Q. 26:221–227], who lacks the power to *do* precisely *because* he claims the power to *say*. He is the self-made, self-spoken, self-fragmented man; he is the Byrthonic god Dylan hurling himself into the waves of the sea to become a cold, silver fish in the moaning, roaring ocean of material existence. Later on, God willing, he will get a chance to be that salmon, "fighting upstream to the Source of his hunger".

The sands, said Eve,
Are those of North Africa. Only the wind distributes
The numerals that compose me, the arid glyphs. Plough and furrow
Died five thousand years ago in these valleys.
The rock of my mountains
Holds the fine bones of fish in silent memory.
I wait for the promise to be fulfilled,

My husband gone so long ago, on his journey to draw water
From the Wells of Aquarius. He said a star would point the way.
Who has seen him? Who gathered news of his troubles?

Where is my husbandman, my beloved?
Where is the rain?

And as Man dissolves in the ocean of psycho-physical chaos, the Earth is
bereft of him; *deserted*; become *desert*. Sodden Poseidon, sinking into his
own depths, leaves Gaia barren and dry. Man, drowning in Nature, is
separated from Nature; Earth, longing for the embrace of Man, drives
him ever further away, into the chaos of his own mind. And so she is
closed to the rain of Mercy.

My name is Light, answered the Alien God: my word, an unbreakable
    cipher,
Sine-wave of white fire on black basalt,
An accurate graph of my structure.
The carved statues of all things,
All I forced into existence to make room for my guarded solitude
Hang there like shields, like arms of my warriors,
Seeded in my blind and
Ringing fire.
None can come to me, no one can find me out
In the house where I live
Because I live in the house of Swiftness.
No thing that breathes has eye to see or ear to follow
The count of that fixed velocity, that nailed emblem
Of absolute duration; only by my sovereign Number can they
    determine
That I am who I am: the rational integer
That burns down all who face me
To worship and white ashes.
I am the incandescent Limit, light in light of which each one sees
Only his own puny shadow thrown against the world
(Each eye broken
In the eye of the Other),
Voice in thunder of which no man's word has power

Beyond the wall of his own tongue—
Because wherever my eye chooses to dawn, all speech is war:
I draw every numbered man
Into the ranks of my book.

And when longing Eve tries to turn back to the Spirit, which she lost when she lost her husband Adam, all that appears is the Law Archon, a counterfeit of God—the Spirit not fertilizing Nature but opposed to her, binding her, beating her down. ("Who unleashed order on the world"? lamented the melancholy Greek girl Maria I met in Berkeley once.) Informing and life-giving Form, veiled, becomes the cruel and inflexible Archon of Law, appearing here as *C*, Einstein's quantitative counterfeit of God the Father—the speed of light as universal constant; this reduction of God to a number and a diagram is the dark side of the Hebrew Kabbalah. Nature, degraded to dead matter, when she turns back to God as the Source of her life—now exiled to the distant sky—can see nothing of God but a scientist tinkering with genes, a bulldozer tearing down the sacred hills, even *Safa* and *Marwa* (now desecrated by the Wahhabis).

(Where all silence is crime and all speech confession
The groan of molten lava is ambiguous to my ear;
The lower populations blow like sand, they heave and surge like
        water;
Hunting is only intermittently productive in the forests of the Empire
Where the seasons jerk and twist like a snake under my hammer —
I hold land. I station garrisons. I cut the Earth into leys and borders.
I distribute the fragments of Adam's mask to my legions, glowing
        chalk of the kiln
Cooled and hardened into the stamped coin of Everyman, my name
        and my image:
Till every man is licensed to whip his own plate of Earth, drive cattle
        into barns, brand his women
With the burning name of the Alien God, as duly financed by lawful
        taxation
To be collected in the coin
Of the human face.

And when the Spirit as Eternal Form is veiled in Man, forcing him in Promethean, Nietzschean, mode to identify himself with God, when he looks out of his cavern upon the wilderness of the world he sees nothing but a brutal, degenerate chaos to be whipped into order. And when he surveys the human race, all he can see is a sullen, rebellious jungle, a field of human weeds.

> I hunt whales. I swim deep into the sea forests,
> Squaring the net of the law against squid and dolphin, sea lion and
>   albacore,
> Till the ocean is a broth of pain.
> I transform the heart's watery canyons
> Into the wards of a penal zoo—whole species,
>   Excised from wilderness,
> Shackled, cowed with drugs
> Stand petrified, like marble statues, bone dry and white under the
> Faltering eyes
> Of the Crowd....
>   (They leap against the
>   bars of their own faces, taste the cool
>   water of their blood and are suddenly
>   docile and translucent.)

But when he goes to war with the elements to rank and order them, he only wounds them, destroys them, and so ultimately falls under their power. The failure of the great crusade of the Law Archon to impose pre-conceived order upon nature—which results only in the destruction of nature's *implicate* order—is lamented by Adam below:

> I would give these two eyes, Adam said
> To see your face again,
> And hold it between these hands—
> That face become all faces now,
> In a bitter storm of memory....

> I would die to know you... relax the blade of my anger
> In soft shade. Dream an hour,

Or a year. To lose this heavy body
Under dripping roots,
In the heave and surge of water,
The ground itself, moving
In slow waves....
I would lay my bones there; I would place my eyes
Deep in your keeping, if that would give me the power
To see that beloved face
Only one more time—for an hour, or a minute —
Before earth and water
Choke this voice.

Adam's dream of return to the lost Eve as the bosom of the natural Earth
is—with the Spirit still veiled—only a dream of death; like Keats, he is
"half in love with easeful death". When the Human Form, known only
as ego, becomes too heavy to bear, a petrified crust, a case of Man
crushed in his own fist, Nature appears as a dream of safety and
freedom—or did to my generation (the last who could see Her like
this?)—but is found, upon close, irreparable inspection, to be nothing
but dissolution—the Chaos Archon. Petrification dreams of Chaos—and
Chaos petrifies.

The thousand rivulets of my blood, answered the Mountain Mother
Are cool water over the fever of your burning body
Which lives only in my memory: The day I was striding through the
    Lunar Forests with Eve my daughter—we drew you, Adam; our
      hands were hungry—
You leapt out of yourself to meet us; you held nothing back.
          So find her now,
In the shifting mazes of the willow or the spikes of the cactus,
Her face dividing into twenty masks, lost in a thicket
Of thorny arteries and bleeding vines....
Or only the brief ripples on a pond, the shifting mirrors of water,
    laddered in section, melting down cool into rock....

The trees billow and heave in the ocean of Air;
One limb sprouts a fish, another a rooster's head;

A third puts out a gnarled, human hand. Earth-phallus mushrooms,
  flecked with seed,
Your belly sucked out thin and white in the
Trickling channels of my form,
The day I wed the forest tree-high, walking in bridal white and
  smooth black skin....
All husbands were my husband then, all sons my son—remember?

Eve, the human soul, is lost now, dispersed in the elements. For Adam
seek her in the Chaos to which she has retreated is only to dismember
her further, to drive her farther into exile. This is the wages of Nature
Worship.

(The ice of your lips on my lips, said Adam, is not cold; it has no
  temperature; it burns like phosphorus.

"And shall I take off my clothes?"
                                        Yes.
    "Fine, and this too?"
                              Yes.
                                  We nod to the Kings and Queens
      of my spine as they rise;
It is a salt minuet, a courtly dance. We sway to the hammer-blows
  of Silence raining down.)

And when he does find her—like the reunion of Ivan and Marichka in
Sergei Parajanov's great motion picture masterpiece *Shadows of our For-
gotten Ancestors*—it is a union only in death; as the Bardo of Experienc-
ing Reality commences [cf. the *Bardo Thödöl*], the shining Archetypes
arise from the decay of the incarnate human form. Yet the ultimate
pathos of that loss is also a foreshadowing of the true Spiritual Death,
and the Wedding Feast for which it is the one garment that guarantees
admittance.

I am a silent flare of Power over a wilderness of mountains, over
  deserts of snow;
I am hammered silver, clotted ash, gullies of frozen light;

[133]

My devotees I leave exposed in lightningflash, breathless and
    panting to step toward heaven;
I am breath of their breath, power of their eyes;
They are nothing but a story retold
Over and over again in the slow circle of my beauty.
I look down quietly on all nakedness, exposing the lovers in their
    beds of seed;
I whisper destinies into the germ plasm and the budding embryo,
Predicting and dictating the count and pattern of the breath,
Done as recorded in the starry college of the midnight sky,
A zoo of glyphs and runes.
I am the terror that comes in the night,
Terror of the mouse, waiting for the owl to cover her, glowing
    faintly violet in the darkness;
I am the cool white nurse with her tray of simples,
Bending over the whirlpool that turns on the bed;
I hold the key to the citadel of electroshock—the roaring white
    Silence
That wipes out all memory of the crime.

But Adam's embrace of Eve in the kingdom of Death is short-lived and
ambiguous. Chaos, pursued (and no man can catch that swift Atlanta; as
Rumi said, "this world is beautiful as a bride, but none can marry that
ravishing one"), finally turns into a fourth Archon: a Goddess of Fate; a
cold, inhuman, starry Destiny; a deathly fascination. The dark, constant
Earth turns lunar at last, changed to the face of the ever-changing
Moon—a fascinating barrenness—a barren fascination. ("The Moon
eats us", G.I. Gurdjieff said.) She is the *hiemarmene* now, a cold, inhu-
man, fatalistic zodiac cut off from the Archetypes of the Intelligible
Plane, the eternal forms of God's merciful Will for all things, and left to
revolve on its own (the Deists saw her like this, though they wouldn't
admit it), like the form of that bladed wheel by which St. Catherine, ser-
vant of Holy Wisdom, was martyred. Wisdom, veiled, is transformed
into Mystery; Providence, veiled, becomes Fate. And as Chaos is death
by dismemberment, so Fate—no less fatal—is death by transformation
into a pillar of salt. It is Fate that torments Chaos—that makes the soul
chaotic, drives it crazy, then punishes it for that very disorder. Likewise

it is Chaos that turns Fate to ice for fear of that all-devouring vortex, that *samsara*; this is the irony of natural, automatic, Furious "justice" in a world without God.

> You were my flesh, Adam said—
> Then that flesh was taken from me.
>
> What did I care
> For the dead meat left,
> This useless anchor
> That sold me into the power of gravity,
> When all I wanted was to fly,
> To leave this place
> As you had left it?
> I could travel anywhere, easily,
> Any point of the compass
> And never find one clear sheet of water
> To return my face to me....
>
> And when I tried to die to get you back,
> When I returned from my journey
>
> To the edge of this world and the
> Blank white face of death,
>
> My own body
> No longer welcomed me home.

When we lose the power to see ourselves in the mirror of God, it seems that the mirror of the Earth is still left to us. But Earth, like Heaven, passes away. God is the Priest Who marries Man and Earth; without the priesthood of God, Earth abandons us. These are the wages of false *psychic* Transcendence, of "grandiose ascent". The head flies free, along Eagle Axis, leaving the body to sink into stunned paralysis. (I once had a dream, after visiting the Philippine psychic surgeons, that a winged being called Eagleaxis ascended with me straight up the Vertical Path, to a darkened, abandoned amphitheater where my dead father sat, drinking whiskey, and refused to acknowledge me as his son.) To obey gravity is to tap the power of gravity; to fight gravity is to fall under the power of it. This is Adam's last human cry—the pit of his fall—the ultimate expression of his loss. But it is also the seed of his final return: this depth of lament has become a cry finally sharp enough to pierce the terrible deafness of God.

You were my burning Sun, said Eve,
But then that sun was darkened.
What could fire mean to me now,
When my thighs and breasts could no
    longer bask
In the light of your voice?

All I wanted was to sink,
To bury myself deeper in my own
Stunned body,
As you had buried yourself
In the impenetrable sky.

I could travel through the whole Earth
    in serpent-form, that was in my power,
On in the form of woody roots twist
    myself deeper—

But where is the Sun that might unlock my
    heart-knowledge—
Or is he dead forever?

I struggled to lift the whole Earth,
Hundreds of miles of olivine mantle
Above my molten core,
And the granite above that—
But fell back

Under the weight of your absence.
The orbit of a cinder around a

Dead star is the
Road I travel,

Through abandoned cities of
Space and time.

Substance without Essence is matter; matter without form is chaos.
When Eve fell, she fell into the earth; when Adam fell, he fell into the sky.

I called upon her
She was not receiving;
She had other business
Behind the door of death.

I said I love you—
She did not answer;
She had pressing business there
Her ear was deaf.

I died to know her
She was glad receiving;
She knew my voice and she
Knew my eyes;

I held her closely
We two were one there;
My voice was softened, earth
Choked my cries.

But union in death is the seed that ripens unto resurrection. "All find
shelter in the tomb", said Yeats. Those destined for resurrection, how-
ever, can find no shelter. Not even death is a sure refuge from love,
because love conquers death—transforms it into a servant, a messenger.

Our real fear
Is not of death:
By the testimony of every ghost

We know our mask survives it.
What we fear most truly
Is love itself.

—because there is a trance in death.
You faint at one point, they say....
And then all fear and hunger
Are equal.

But in love,
Death only sharpens everything.
Blood grows in radiance.
Every sense is clarified,
Every faculty enlightened.
The fluted mask
Of the face is shattered.
You watch—having no longer any way
     to close your eyes—
How every cell in your body
Is exquisitely, mercilessly
Brought to birth.
Oblivion does not guard this gate
As it does the gate to the womb;
The chest is torn open,
And what rises to the eyes, black and red,
Like water rising in a broken ship
Is not sleep—it is Light. Death
Is only a precarious, temporary refuge
From a light like that.
The soul runs from tomb to tomb,
Praying for a little shelter,
Pounding on stone slabs with
     fists of air—
And how deaf they are, with their
     carved smiles,
With their beards of moss.
A blind hawk does not escape the dawn:

He suffers it. Hell
Is the measure of resistance;
A loving hand, laid on breast or shoulder
The measure of defeat.

As the Eastern Orthodox theologians say, Hell is not first an expression
of Divine Wrath, but of God's Love—which the prideful, passion-rid-
den ego can only experience as Hellfire. The "defeat" is the defeat of the
ego, the self-will. God *is* Love; the ego *is* Hell.

Who will write the history
Of the post-human age
The days we occupy,
When human flesh was only an unsettled
    memory
Nagging the archives?

Will the Doomsday Vault that contains the seeds of all humanly-useful
plants, preserved against ecological destruction, ultimately also contain
the Human Genome? Like the Zoroastrian Var of Yima, the under-
ground compound which preserves the seed of the best plants, the best
animals, the best human beings while the Apocalypse passes over?—
Yima, like Adam, being the First Prophet, both Man Alpha and Man
Omega?

Who will name the thing that so profoundly
    terrified us
That we begged to be made machines of
To hide from the face of it?
                                        (I will:
    It was *love*).

I might or might not have been the first to coin the term "post-human";
in any case, others have now come upon the same phrase—inevitably so.

There is no home for us now
    say the sons of Hawking, the wise of this world

                       but endless space, the
Dark Mother—
(We are *contained* in Her, sunk in black,
                  swarming emptiness—
      Can't you feel it?
        Our conceptual universe "finite yet unbounded" now,
             like the womb is, which means
    That we haven't even been born yet—
     We are still INSIDE Her, held within
     invisible walls of Cosmos.
  We wander down roads of our Mother,
    through gales of energy,
    past galaxies of stars, longing
      with the deepest powers of matter itself
to break the light barrier, to reverse the flow of time....
    we are groping, stumbling back to our childhood in
vast Machines,
       into the Black Hole, the concentrated
        Hunger of space—

A universe conceived of as capable of existing without God, as nothing more than a material object, is a self-enclosed system—a womb. In such a universe, every attempt to reach "escape velocity", to "slip the surly bonds of earth", to transcend material limitations by strictly material means, is ultimately an attempt to return to the womb—and this remains the case even when that return is couched in the most triumphal Promethean terms. This is one of the supreme ironies of the modern scientistic worldview: that the Promethean/adolescent rebellion against Mother Earth simply feeds the foolish young titan of triumphal scientism, piece by piece, into the Maw of Mother Space. Einsteinian and post-Einsteinian cosmology sees the universe as without edge or boundary— *as if* it were infinite—but as finite in fact; in this it is precisely equivalent to an intra-uterine existence. Both the universe's lack of boundary and its inescapable finitude are reflections of our identification with it—an identification which scientism, it its denial of God, renders inevitable. If the material universe is all there is, then it must be infinite—particularly since there is nothing outside it. But in fact it is *not* infinite. Its imagined infinity reflects the complacency of our identification with it, just as its actual finitude reflects the despair inherent in that complacency—despair and complacency (the archonic counterfeits of Awe and Hope) being inseparable partners in all matter-worship, whether its object be a Nature Goddess in rebellion against transcendence, against God the Father, or the mere belief in, and reliance upon, raw material quantity.

BACK—

before birth—

before spacetime unfolded its flower—

into a Bardo of buzzing Energy—

KALI!

KALI!

Under sodium pentathol, the clattering sounds of the operating room sped up (as my brain slowed down) till they became the high-pitched metallic whine of Death: of form unveiled as Energy. (The Tibetans understand this transmutation of form into vibration as one of the stages of the death-process; their deep, base, polyphonic chanting, filled with high-pitched harmonics, is designed to bring the unconscious memory of this universal, underlying condition of things into full consciousness.) When the Absolute dawns not as trans-formal Essence manifesting as eternal Form, but as universal Substance manifesting as the dissolution of all forms into primal Energy (this being the inevitable end of the materialistic conception of things)—that is Kali.

According to René Guénon in *The Reign of Quantity and the Signs of the Times*, the final end of materialism, which effects an actual petrification of the cosmic environment, rendering it opaque to the light of higher realities, is for this petrified environment to crack, shatter, and ultimately dissolve, leading to the end of this world, this cycle-of-manifestation. Early in the cycle, according to Guénon, Form or Essence has precedence over Matter or Substance, while at the end of the cycle, in the Kali-yuga, Substance (as metaphysical principle) and Matter (as the outward expression of that principle) predominate, and ultimately triumph.

This, again, is Kali.

You who were never born and will never die,
Who stand in your high tower and look out
Over the lands and cities of Your own eternity,
How can You understand us here, nagged by the shadow of death, in
  mortal space and time?

You *are* that; you are My knowledge of you.

You Who are made of nothing but the bliss of Your own nature, and
  know that bliss as Truth,
What can You know of our great suffering here? How can You feel
  our pain?
What can You understand of an incandescent cloud of human souls
  over Hiroshima, ovens of holocaust smelting a fine ash of bone in
  the alchemy of Antichrist,
Of Timur the Lame and his mountain of human eyes?

You *are* that; you are My knowledge of despair and agony.

You Who are made of nothing but the Truth of Your own nature, and
  know that Truth as bliss,
What can You understand of lies and illusions? Whatever is real is
  purely Yourself; whatever is unreal has never existed.
What can You know of the battle of Truth against illusion, of a
  knowledge that is not only Bliss, but also Justice?

**You *are* that; you are My knowledge of war. And your knowledge
  of Me, that whatever is real is purely Myself, that whatever is
  unreal has never existed—**
That is your sword.

You Who know nothing but Your own infinite Radiance, Light that
  swallows the universe and us along with it
As if we never drew breath—what can You know of tiny worlds: a
  favorite street, a favorite tree,
A beloved wife or husband, a little house, a little child?

You *are* that knowledge; you are My delegated Eye on the
    infinitesimal mountains and plains of My existence.
Through you I know them as created; through Myself I know them
    as Myself alone,
Who devours the universe as fire consumes a forest,
As a rose-window gathers its fragments, magnetizing them to a new
    design
Of crystallized flame.
You know I create you only to destroy you; the clock you made
So testifies. Only I know that I create you in the very act of that
    destruction,
Ruthlessly annihilating the lie that you are self-begotten, tearing
    down the last wall that would prevent Me
From walking alive in your flesh, speaking with your voices and
    looking out through your eyes.

Hadith qudsi: "My slave ceaseth not to draw near unto me by devotions
of his free will until I love him; and when I love him, I am the hearing
whereby he heareth and the sight whereby he seeth and the hand where-
with he smiteth and the foot whereon he walketh."

This is how I gather the galaxies and starclusters home to My
    Secret, through My Eye which opens in the human heart
At the command of My Messengers. And the pith of their message
Is that man never fell. You see yourself as exiled from My
    threshold, born into a self-subsistent world, a sky that doesn't
    know you.

If the Fall of Man is a fall from Eternity into time and from Truth into
illusion, then, in one sense, that Fall is itself an illusion — an illusion with
very real, and terrible, consequences. Only if Man, in his deepest
essence, remains unfallen, can the effects of the Fall be reversed; as the
Zen practitioners say, "If you want to be Enlightened, first you have to
be Enlightened."

Through your eye, I see what you see. Through My Eye
On the surface of which your vision floats,
Chip of wood on a shoreless ocean,

> I see Myself Alone. This is the rigor of My judgement,
> And My Mercy that overwhelms and drowns that rigor.
> From the secret form of Man within me, whose essence is Woman;
> From Adam the mystery of My self-knowledge
> And Eve My veiled and My naked Truth,

The reality of God's Self-knowledge is the Primordial Adam, the eternal archetype of the human form—in Christian terms, the Second Person of the Blessed Trinity, Christ being "the second Adam". In the world of creation, the transcendent, masculine, personal God—the very face of that Divine Self-knowledge—takes precedence over feminine Nature; He is Her Ruler; She is His manifestation, His *Shekhina*, His *Shakti*. But in the world of the Unseen, the Divine Essence, or Beyond Being, Which is feminine—symbolized in Christianity by the Black Virgin and by the Sufis as Layla—takes precedence over the Personal God, or Pure Being, Who is masculine; She is His Matrix, His secret Essence. Eve, veiled, is the visible cosmos; Eve, naked, is the Virgin Mary, hidden in the depths of the Divine Nature.

> The seven rays of My Mercy shine down into your mistaken world,
> Into the belief that you are self-created, that the threads of your
>   origin are lost in the wilderness
> Of matter, energy, space and time.
> My Mercy is Virgin, Torah, Qur'an: invisible sister, a lost world
> Walking beside you, in daily and accepted sorrow:
> Deep-forgotten vigilance
> Spying on your sleep.

Even though we are asleep, the Knowledge of God is awake within us. May we awaken to that Knowledge, and rise up from this world of dreams.

> Remember Her—one death your whole payment—and I will
>   remember you.

THREE

In the Cave of the Heart shines a hot, interior Sun.

This is the Uncreated Intellect; the *Ruh*; the *Nous*; the Eye of the Heart. As the outer world expands and dissipates to its destruction, the inner world gathers and concentrates until it reaches the point of incandescence—like a star being born—and the Eye of the Heart is unveiled.

Sometimes it is veiled by leaden clouds,

The Fate Archon

Sometimes by a mist of dull, tarnished gold.

The Law Archon

At times the clouds are a muddy olive color;

The Chaos Archon—the froggy, green, artistic jealousy of the Collective Unconscious

At other times, the color of dried blood.

The Archon of Promethean Selfhood

But beyond the veils of despair and complacency,
Of shapeless intoxication and grim spiritual will

These are the four dispositions of the will and the affections proper to the archons of Fate, Law, Chaos and Selfhood respectively, they who are the elementals of the human ego, the four most fundamental and primordial misperceptions of the nature of God.

A find gold Sun is roaring with knowledge
Over an incandescent ocean, heaving in mountains of divine
energy,

The tidal-waves of the Aeons: passing as we watch them
But eternal in the Core of radiance, before whose face
We rise, and pass, like voices. Whatever word is heard in that
    light
Stands like a pillar
Between earth and sky.

Again, the Uncreated Intellect, whose Light is the Logos, the world-cre-
ating Shout. In Eternity, every world is an age, every age a world; the
Greek word for both is *aion*. Time flows there, but it does not pass. The
vast Archangels who are the eternal forms of the passing ages stand as
eternal Words of God, the established pillars of His Kingdom. In our
incarnate forms we are brief, fleeting, ephemeral in relation to them, like
wisps of smoke; in our discarnate forms, we *are* them. (This vision came
to me via the *ajña-chakra* trance kindly provided to visitors, free of
charge, by Brahma Kumaris of San Francisco, California.)

In relation to the Substantial Pole, the light of the Intellect becomes
the creative wind of the Spirit; *Nous* becomes *Pneuma*, the Spirit of God
that moved on the face of the waters. The power to know that something
is, reflected on a lower level, is the power to make something *be*.

So now the Violet Fear and the White Fear.
Now the full Beast driven from the heart, rising in front of us,
And us knowing him.

Open Hell. Seal not the door where evil dwells.
Stir the banked coals, the immemorial anger, the mirror-bound
    suicides,
    Lizards on a red cliff at dawn...they flex the sinews of their wings,
    They take delight in their own beings....

The Violet Fear is the fear of death; the White Fear is the fear of Tran-
scendence. The unveiling of the Presence of God in the midst of a fallen
world, a world that has sealed itself against Him and denied Him in
every particular, initiates Apocalypse for that world. In the macrocosm,
the advent of the Kalki Avatara, the Messiah, the Eschatological Christ
catalyzes the resurrection of the dead; what Christ's harrowing of Hell

did for Sheol, the return of the Messiah will do for this world now become no better than Sheol: the righteous will be freed from their captivity, and the wicked cast into a lake of fire. Likewise, in the microcosm, the unveiling of the Eye of the Heart, which is the Real Presence of God in the human soul, initiates the resurrection of all that has been dead in that soul, all the unactualized potentials and the karmic residues of past actions, good, evil or neutral. That Presence is the Star that falls from Heaven at the fifth trumpet of the Apocalypse, and opens the bottomless pit [Rev. 9:1], as well as the "day star" that will "arise in your hearts" [Peter 1:19].The "Hell" opened here, then, is not the Hell of eternal damnation, but the Hades of all that has been denied the chance to undergo Judgement and Purgation. In the words of Blake, "When a man rejects Error and embraces Truth, a Final Judgement passes upon that man." A Theosophical Society invocation petitions whatever power the Theosophists worship that it might "seal the door where evil dwells." Insofar as this indicates a will to avoid or deny the Judgement of God, it must be reversed; it is reversed here. Satan must be loosed so that he may fulfill his destiny as both an agent and a recipient of Divine Judgement. The "mirror-bound suicides" are those who killed their spiritual potential by sacrificing it to their self-image in the mirror of the ego. Will their self-delight return them to the Divine Self within them? Or will it bind them to their false selves forever? Only Judgement knows the answer.

I say all will be pressed into service.
I say all will be required to fight.
The passive, the coward, the innocent will be trampled down,
Unless locked in single combat with Antichrist
In mountain solitude and stillness.

Invoke, therefore, the war in your marrow;
Call on the fight you were born with, that enemy
Whose lie is cut and tooled, precisely,
To cover your single truth.
Pick targets. Each man is alone with all men
In this night of war. The conglomerate form of Death
Stands guard on each human door,

Solid to the bullet, and the chisel—like those cliffs in the Sinai
In which our skirmishers discovered, still living
The imprisoned forms of men!

Judgement is the separation of the sheep from the goats, the greater
jihad. While we are still alive in this world we are not *passive* to God's
Judgement; that superlatively *active* call commands us to enter into the
agon of revelation, and into the purgation that comes with it, so as to free
the Human Form from its sub-human prison in the wilderness of the elements. All that is dead in us must die; all that is alive in us must go to Life
Eternal. And since Intellect has ontological precedence over Will in the
spiritual anthropology of the Human Form, this purgation is *first* a war
against error in the name of Truth, and *lastly* a war against sin in the
name of Sanctity.

The sky is roofed with machines now, a guarded perimeter to
block out the angelic orders;

Where once we raised our eyes to the heavens, hoping for a vision of
God and His angels, the shreds of the Divine Human Imagination can
now see only quasars, or black holes, or the Global Positioning System—
the forms taken by the Universal Divine Witness under Scientism and
the Reign of Quantity.

The earth is filled with the limbs of struggling giants, locked apart
in separate mirrors, in cold branching corridors of time;
They are powers of creation chained in elemental caverns when
the Human Form was planted on earth,
Because Man, when he fell, needed ground under his feet, the
bedrock of God—

The Giant Living Forms of the previous cycle of manifestation have
become the *materia* and *potentia* of the present cycle, "the Antediluvians
who are our Energies" (Blake, from *The Marriage of Heaven and Hell*),
just as the forests and dinosaurs of past biological ages have become the
coal and petroleum of our own Kali-yuga. When all that potential is
finally actualized, when all that fuel is finally burned, the end of this age
will come.

[148]

But we have forgotten God now, and the rock is unsteady; our
     foundations crack like parchment, they heave and shift like
     water;
The mechanical chatter of demons, the acid of shattered images
     are our gods and our protectors;
The wasp and the locust advise us; the spider and the scorpion
     guard our sleep.

Once Earth was recognized as the Cave of the Holy Ancestors who are
the Names and Seeds of every human child born under the sun. But if the
Dead are no longer known as alive in their own world—if the blue vil-
lage of the living is no longer situated just over the next rise from the
purple village of the dead—then Form deserts Matter entirely, and Mat-
ter dissolves. And in the process, the human soul sinks till it comes to
resemble the souls of insects, in that day when *mankind will be as thickly-
scattered moths* [Q. 101:4], worshipping the elemental click and hum of
quantum indeterminacy.

Who knows this? Who has the courage not to worship
At the feet of his own destroyers?
Friends, I know you.

They are the Remnant—the Remnant of all Revelations and all Times.

You are those scourged by what you see in the crackle and hiss of
     fire
That flowers in the rift of God. You have incontrovertible reason,
     proof to silence laughter.
You are the face of the Divine Humanity, driven to the margins
     and borders of the Earth,
Weighted and crushed by the Trust, till you release the burden of
     your heavy word, to the pavement, to the center of the Earth if
     necessary
That the heart give up her dead;

The Word that is released to sink to the center of the Earth is Christ har-
rowing Hell; and the Great Star of Rev. 9:1; and the Trust spoken of in

Q. 33:72: Lo! We offered the Trust to the heavens and the earth and the hills, but they shrank from bearing it and were afraid of it; and Man assumed it. Lo! he hath proved a tyrant and a fool.

> You walk through the cities of the grave in the high mountains
>   with food and intelligence for your people;

In this night of war we no longer know the names of our allies, our brothers and sisters; we fight side-by-side with total strangers who are closer to us than our own blood kin.

> You open your throats to the Messengers to give them a living
>   voice;
> Saints take council beneath your ribs;

The Qur'an in the written letter is a tomb of the holy dead; on the human tongue, it is the living Word of God, incandescent and brief, like lightning. It comes. It is gone. It comes again. With each flash, inside each reverberating cloak of darkness, the universe is created. And annihilated. And created again.

> You offer your bodies to be the purgatory
> Of souls you will never know.

The apocalypse and purgation of the macrocosm is worked out, in spiritual mode, within the microcosm. To the degree that we are purified, through purgatorial suffering, of our own errors and vices, we inherit the errors and vices of the whole world, and let them be worked out *through* us. To the degree that we are without sin, crucifixion and vicarious suffering are inevitable; the Bodhisattva Vow is not a choice, but an inescapable consequence of Awakening. And insofar as we recognize our suffering as being, in reality, not our own suffering but the suffering of the God within us, then it is, in essence, no suffering.

> You are those who in your hunger did not ask for food and so
>   became storehouses;
> Who in thirst did not cry for water and so became rivers;

Who in nakedness did not flinch under shame, but suffered it,
    rejecting the cloth of the world,
And so became a city for all people, where no-one is refused

Vicarious suffering is for more than Christ, just as Christ is of more than
Jesus. To suffer the essential pain of existence consciously, without com-
plaint or rationalization or recoil, or the longing for sleep, is to ease the
suffering of all sentient beings. Buddha *is* Bodhisattva, intrinsically. To
awaken *is* to save.

But only those who know how to place their foreheads on the
    dusty earth
Can enter.

Prostration is annihilation; *sajda* is *fana*. Annihilation is the key to that
city, since it is harder for a rich man to enter the Kingdom of Heaven
than for a camel to pass through the eye of a needle—the term for a nar-
row gate into a Near Eastern city that required pack camels to be
relieved of their cargo before they could pass through (the cargo being
the ego). Spiritual War is, finally, all Surrender; the human will is com-
pletely free and whole only at that moment when it is intentionally sur-
rendered to the Will of God.

You live in that Year
When each man and woman picks up their whole cross and
    walks,
In the terrible sunrise, down the burning road,
As the structure of consensus reality crashes around us,
Torn free from the flesh of memory,
Stripped naked to Mercy,
Gone beyond Death—

And that Surrender is not over and done with in the first scene of the first
act; Surrender must be renewed with each step on the Path, with each
conscious breath. And what must be surrendered is precisely This
World—the collective origin of the Ego—and the Ego—the individual
origin of This World: they are one and the same. Both the World and the

Ego are guarded by Memory, and Memory is the Enemy of true Remembrance, the Warden of Unredeemed Karma, the Tomb of Eternal Death. Remembrance destroys Memory, that perishing world, and admits us to the Court of the King.

> The scythe reaps, the seed-heads fall
> The harvest barn is hidden everywhere in the fire;
> And the wedding-smoke rises,
> Perfume of all love and murder,
> Heroism, quite secret work
> In the caverns of the heart,
> Pounding the stone doors
> Of those sacrificial priests
> Who desecrate the Human Form to build the regime of Antichrist,
> Gods of the New World Order,
> Powers of frigid glamour, and insane false hope, and numb
>   despair:
> Pour fire against their sanctuary,
> Against the Dragon
> Against the Tower—
> Glyphs of destiny, strung like nets
> Through the charged structure of the thunderhead
> Weave lightning into working knowledge,
> Where the Living Truth sits mounted and armed
> In the region of the Air, on the borders of the next world now shining
>   into this one, in dream and vision more solid than a rock in the hand,
> To overturn their altars, those blissful devotees, worshippers of
>   despair incarnate
> To whom Love is a torturing fire.
> At the precise point where their pain and loss are most deeply denied,
> In the mouth of their wisest wound these words are engraved
> White fire cut on black fire on the
> Skeletal plasm of their nerves:
> And Love is what we wish them.
> But how can they accept such a gift from the likes of us?
> How can they even know their need?
> They are inheritors of the whole world—we are nothing
> But inheritors of the earth.

All true love, and suffering, and work, and battle will be requited, even if they never once appeared in the streets of this world. Love is a Wedding; that Wedding is a Sacrifice; and that Sacrifice will accomplish its object: to tear down the citadel of the ego, both individual and collective, that masquerades as God, to overturn the total regime of lies and lovelessness and deathly cold, which is the Kingdom of Antichrist. The war against the forces of evil begins with righteous anger, but the rigors of that war lead on to an irreversible escalation, until finally the Ultimate Weapon is deployed: *love itself.*

So in the beginning we are walking over a half-barren field
That is the bones of the dead.
From here, God is a tower of fire —vines of light rising in scales of
    granite and diamonds
Up his thighs of forests and cataracts, tangled limbs of giants in the
    hills,
Studded with a million flowers, irises and poppies, vibrating in the
    wind
Of a precise and endless language....

His belly is the ocean, acrid with iodine, moaning with great whales,
Filled with the darting silver arrows of sentience, the tides of ancient
    feeling
That empower the biological universe....

While on the peaks of the mountains His eagles perch and soar, scanning
    the wars of His intelligence,
The burning white sky above, streaming with the rays of His hair, the
    black mazes of the night, the firing synapses of the stars....

The Divine Immanence unveiled: in the Presence of God all things are annihilated in their separate identities; all things *are* that Presence.

And from here, God is a man and a woman, locked in pounding
    embrace,
Revolving with eyes and fingers, surrounded by the archangels of their
    children,
The Lion, the Bull, the Eagle and the Man, planets turning in deep space
    on a solid wheel of light,

Crystalline chariot of the Almighty shifting dimensions as music,
The living shape, in eternity, of the human body itself: a Wheel—
Where gulfs of fire and hurtling stones are succulent fruits on the
     Tree of Life,
Whose roots are invisible, beyond measure, beyond science, beyond
     time and space, sunk in the earth of Eden;
Whose branches, visible and invisible, are towers of vision, where the
     eye sees itself nowhere
But at the back of the mirror, among corridors of radiance, torrents of
     vitality, arteries of silence,
Fleet mercuries in the metabolism of God,
Whose word is Vortex, Star, Warp, magnetic Flux,
Whose word is Mouse, Bear, Bison, Eagle, the guardian beasts,
Reverberating from the fiery shield of the Angelic Orders
In Space and Light, Sublime Pen and Guarded Tablet,
     they who shield with their hands
Trembling human birds in the nest of the lone destroyer, naked
Before the vastness of God....

The total unveiling of God's Immanence annihilates the "old heaven and
the old earth" in the One Reality—which immediately re-polarizes as
"the new heaven and the new earth", Shiva and his Shakti, Source and
Manifestation, and the entire Hierarchy of Being that is the full deploy-
ment of that manifestation; the very destruction of the Universe *creates*
the universe, inevitably. It is the Great Chain of Being as *veil* that pro-
tects us from the direct Light of God, which would immediately annihi-
late us, just as it is that same Chain as *revelation* which transmits to us the
Light by which we live.

And SHE says: I am Black Space hugging motionless swiftness.

And HE says: I am Light pouring myself through space as music.

And SHE says: I am the spiral Void, the close grain of darkness.

And HE says: I am absolute velocity—step once into my river, you are
     motionless in the core of Radiance.

And SHE says: I am Universe, Black Rose wounded with starlight;

> my necklace of children is strung on a bullet's line
> among these jeweled arrows of the Night—

I am the hunger for Truth, I know all: I am the Truth itself, I know
nothing.
We are the circulation of the living Word, the eternal loud Cry
generating universe forever,
Radiating our ancestors and children throughout the six directions of
time and space,
From whom you've picked the loveliest of our daughters, the blue one,
Spenta Armaiti, Angel of the Earth, to be your sister,

Spenta Armaiti is the Earth Angel of the Zoroastrians, who see the Earth
not as a Goddess but as a sentient being, an organism with a beginning
and an end, but one who possesses, like all sentient beings, an eternal
aspect, a *soul*.

Bathed in the living furnace of the Sun—
Named her as Humanity's chosen seat in the six-dimensional signature
of Eternity,
Where past and future, two rivers, empty their cargoes forever into the
clear well of the moment,
Into a Paradise found, lifted from exile, held between our two hands,
Alive in the crystal chalice
Of the human eye.

The Earth is not our home by chance or accident; she is our Emanation,
our Shakti, the material and subtle-energetic expression of the very soul
of the Human Form; from her alone proceed the three axes and six direc-
tions of space as deployed by God's first agents of creation, the six-
winged Seraphim. On the Moon, on Mars, in the emptiness of interplan-
etary space, we cannot be fully human. As we witness her by the Divine
Witness within us, pre-eternity and post-eternity are united with, and in,
the Present Moment; the Earth returns to her perfect prototype in the
Mind of God. And when the Earth enters eternity, all the dead held
within her arise from that death, and live.

The horn of remembrance now cracks the shell

Encrusted on the heart for six thousand years,
Awakening the nations of the human dead
From their iron sleep. The people of the tombs arise and have their
    say
On the plains of Akhirah:

Akhirha is the Arabic/Quranic term for the Next World.

                        "We are those
Who lie slandered under the name of death.
We have incontrovertible reason,
Proof to silence laughter.
From palaces of torture,
From twenty terms in the grey, damp, infinite dusk
We raise our voices and salute you,
Who still sit laboring in your dream—
You living men and women, clothed as we were
In the sweetness and the dignity
Of human flesh. We are the strength of your arms and your loins,
The voice of your living memory.
Speak us, man! Tell our story.
We've been muttering too long in our ruined halls, those narrow
    beds,
The groves still barren of our voices;
We've lain too long in the seed-houses, the uneasy archives,
    the crucibles of sleep.
Beware! The dead are hungry for those who will not live;
The ones who die into a coward's dream we consume;
We eat, and are not satisfied.
But as you remember Him, He will also remember us, in our chambers
    of darkness
Till the river of our endless dying flows East again,
Toward the rising sun."

As soon as we catch a whiff of Eternity, the dead begin to blink and
mumble in their sleep. If we catch a real glimpse of it, they awaken and
sit up. But if, instead of becoming established in the vision of Eternity,
we become fascinated with the dark grandeur of the Dead, the Ances-

tors—just as we may become fascinated and abducted by the lower realms of Security, Pleasure and Power that the rising *kundalini* opens up—then we will become one of them, thereby losing salvation both for them and for ourselves; this is precisely one of the greatest spiritual dangers of the art of poetry.

> The Giant of the human dead
> Now rises into the flesh of the Giant of the Living
> Who awakens into Eternal Humanity,
> All sexual music constellated, no human syllable lost—
> His knee parts the Atlantic—he struggles, tears the earth—
> He speaks with our voices, looks out through our eyes,

But if we resist this temptation—if, like Orpheus, we refuse the food of the underworld—then the Dead will rise and constellate as the effective Power of Enlightenment within us, the Serpent Power, the *kundalini*. When the *kundalini* awakens and rises, the *koshas*, the skins-within-skins that make up the human ego, are shed, one by one.

And his word is:

> "All hells are hells of the imagination,
> Because the state of mind that creates the sin
> Also creates the retribution.

These three lines are directly from a dream I had, probably at the age of sixteen. I—as William Blake—was sitting in an amphitheater-like classroom that reminded me of an actual classroom in Marin Catholic High School. Below at the podium, lecturing, was a professorial, bespectacled serpent. Then William Blake/myself rose, and shouted down to him: *"All hells are hells of the imagination, because the state of mind that creates the sin also creates the retribution!"* At this the Serpent Professor breathed fire, and by so doing released many souls from Hell.

> So remember God in the eye of this moment
> And stand free from the Fire.
> The seed of earth
> Is planted in the kingdom of dream;

[157]

The seed of dream
Grows up in the kingdom of vigil.
The portrait is burned
To give recourse to the mirror;
The mirror is broken
To grant precedence to the face.
Whoever you thought you were
Has no place in that court, and this
Is the end of war."

In Vedantic terms, this is the divestiture of the *koshas*—body, feeling, thought, intellect and bliss—the relative and contingent sheathes of the Absolute Witness. Separate identity, held and asserted, is the principle of all conflict—but when the Witness dis-identifies with the *koshas*, they dissolve. They were never there. This is *Shanti*, the Great Peace.

Then Adam, who is the Human Form
Entered the royal palace
And knelt in the Shadow of the King:

"Here are earth's treasures."

These treasures are here already; they have always been with Us in
the guarded vaults.
If they had not been here already, you could never have secured
them.
If you had not labored to secure them, they would not be here
already:
Your work and your practical wisdom
Adorn our court.

"Here are the freed captives."

The freed captives are here already, my advisors and companions.
If they had not been here already, you could never have freed
them.
If you had not fought and suffered to free them, they would not be
here waiting for you;

Your courage and compassion
Make our reign illustrious in every land.

"Then here are wounds, the trophies of war."

Here your wounds are healed—you never received them: Look at
   your hands and your feet!
If they had ever happened in this world
You would never have known the honor of receiving them in that
   world;
If you had shrunk from receiving them in that world
They would be here waiting for you in this world, every one of them:
   Shame
Before the face of eternity.

"So I rest in your good pleasure."

From the point of view of time, intent and destiny are polarized; from
the point of view of Eternity, intent and destiny and one. What in pass-
ing time is a lifetime of experiences and choices, in Eternity is a single
eternal form, enthroning a single, complex, sovereign choice, a timeless
choice like that of the angels, who chose to obey or disobey God "before
time began." But because of the nature of Eternity, which underlies the
moments of our lives rather than simply coming before or after them,
this eternal choice does not negate free will; it does not strictly predeter-
mine our daily choices in passing time, since it can with equal validity be
seen as the final sum of them.

No silence without truth,
No truth without speech....
And no speech without silence.

The silence of self-annihilation conceives God in the soul; God must
manifest because it is the nature of the Truth to communicate itself; and
only self-annihilation can receive the fullness of that communication.

The mouse returns to her nest in the
   tall grass;

The eagle dives into the Sun.
In the roar of God's Silence
The speech of His heraldic beasts
  is heard
Exactly as it is:
In the heart of that Silence
Whoever listens
Becomes all Word.

At the end of time, form is reabsorbed into Essence and matter into Substance. Simultaneously, Essence and Substance are re-polarized; Essence becomes the wave-form, and Substance the wave-medium, of the primal Vibration of the Logos that manifests the Universe; the prototype of this universal manifestation is the *mandala* of the Four Living Creatures. God's eternal Word is the subtlest possible vibration; in terms of the human microcosm, the psycho-physical nervous system, it is the Inner Sound, "the sound of silence". To listen to the sound of that Silence silences our sub-vocal speech, and with it our ongoing habitual act of unconscious self-definition. And when we stop defining ourselves—in other words, when we stop acting as if we were self-created—then we know ourselves as created and maintained in existence by God, instant by instant. We know God as the Speaker, and ourselves as His Words.

The galaxies turn on the
Pivot of a forgotten Name,

When the Name of God enters the spiritual Heart, that Heart is unveiled as the Center of all things. But when that Name is forgotten, then the Center is projected into the wilderness of dimensional existence, imagined to be elsewhere, but never reliably located, never really found. To be centered in the Name is to know that the Center is everywhere, and therefore *here*—closer to us than our jugular vein.

Until that day
When the song of ancient starlight
Rises to the purgatory of
  vishuddha-chakra,
The lotus of the human voice,

And pours back our stolen knowledge
Into the womb of the Essence;
When by the Sun under our breast-bone
We remember the name of our Origin,
And rise, dripping, from the river of
　　human language,
And start emanating from the
　　Throne itself.

Vishuddha-chakra is the throat center in Hindu yoga, the center of mental, reflected knowledge, as mediated by human speech. When we know ourselves as words of God, we know our own speech as a reverberation of His primal Word. Consequently our speech becomes *inspired*; we know it as *breathed into* us, and our separate identity as an egoic illusion, an instance of identity theft. That's when we understand that our Muse is really God, the only Listener, the only One we can ever truly speak to. And so, bleeding fiery words, we begin to return all we are, all the syllables of which we are composed, to their Divine Origin.

　　Human speech, however—no matter how inspired—is endless; it can never be finished with on its own plane. But when the Eye of the Heart opens, that's when we stop being speakers, and know ourselves as *spoken* instead, as emanations of the Logos, the Throne of God. The many words we speak are now synthesized as the single word we *are*.

All things return to Truth, but not through time.
Each moment rises in smokes of holocaust
To unload its harvest of mercy or wrath, vigilance or heedless-
　　ness
On the shores of God.
Ages rise and fall like breath, moving through the lungs
Of a vast Human Form, printed in stars
On the black curtain of the sky:
They breathe in Mercy, and live;
They speak His Name, and die.
And whether the harvest is all the love and fear,
The labor and hidden heroism and secret despair
Of an entire planet, or the crop of a single instant
Of presence, or willed exile,

The scythe falls, the grain and the chaff are separated
Only in this moment.
We stand on the ground of Judgement.
Day faces night in the same sky.
Paradise and the Fire are near.

The Qur'an [2:210] says, *Unto God are all matters returned*. But the universe does not spiritually evolve until it becomes God (as Teilhard de Chardin heretically taught), nor does it contract again in a "Big Crunch" after the "Big Bang" is spent, until it again becomes a single point. It returns to God only through human spiritual attention, which lives in the Eternal Now—or else fails of that return through human heedlessness.

> The greatest beauty
> Is the beauty of the Invisible.
>
> There's nowhere to turn
> To take hold of
> Or behold it.
>
> Like a smell,
> It comes from somewhere beyond directions.
>
> You find it
> By being the place
> In which you've always known it.

How can Beauty be invisible? Didn't Plato say that Beauty is the Splendor of the True, its radiant manifestation? But God's Secret is necessarily more beautiful than anything that can be seen. If it were not, by what power could He call us back to Him out of the wilderness of dimensional existence?

> *Layla*—that's just what she's like.
> Her name has to be Night,
> Because the light of day, unless it falls
> On some mote of dust that
> Thinks it has a name,
> Is black as midnight.

"Layla" means "night" in Arabic. To the Sufis the maiden Layla, lover of Majnun ("madman", literally "jinn-possessed") in Nizami's romance, is a symbol of the Essence of God that cannot be grasped by any intelligence, human or angelic; the attempt to grasp It instead of being grasped *by* It produces madness. The Essence, which is Infinite Light, is darkness to the eyes of all sentient beings; it manifests only *as* those beings, not *to* them. Thus is why Ibn al-'Arabi taught that when one sees oneself in the Mirror of the Essence, it's time to stop—one has reached the highest station.

> Night is Qur'an—night
> And all the stars.
> The stars are the Book,
> But night is the Mother of the Book.

The Mother of the Book is the Celestial Qur'an, only a tiny fragment of which descended to earth as the spoken and written Qur'an. The Mother of the Book is the infinite ensemble of the Thoughts or Words of God, the prototype of universal manifestation. And here the Mother of the Book is further identified with the Essence—not those Thoughts or Words themselves, but the Silence that conceives them, listens to them, and functions as their Matrix.

> She divests herself, when the recitation is ended;
> Undoes the strings of existence
> And drops it, like a robe.

> When the lights went out
> In the great banquet-hall
> Where all the people I had ever known
> Or ever would know
> Were being entertained after dinner
> By the two black-faced *fuqara*
> Directing the spectacle
> Of death and resurrection,

> That was Her. Ever since that night

I have been a slave
Of the unseen beauty.

According to a *hadith* (tradition) of the Prophet Muhammad, peace and blessings be upon him, true dreams—dreams sent by God—constitute "the forty-sixth part of prophecy." The cycle of prophecy began with the prophet Adam and closed with Muhammad; after him, what remains of the prophetic function manifests only in dreams.

I dreamed this dream when I was maybe five years old. It shows the entire pattern of my life, and predicts my entry into Islam, which took place when I was forty. Whenever my life enters a new phase I return to this dream, and always see something in it that I never saw before. Here is the dream:

> I am in a large, luxurious cubical room, paneled in dark brown wood. On each wall is a square of red wallpaper, like cloth, as if it were made of red satin. Each square leaves only a foot or two of the wood paneling of each wall visible, surrounding it on all four sides.

> This room is entered through glass doors on the right-hand wall, beyond which I have a vague sense of a traffic-filled street. I have apparently come into the room through these doors.

> In this room are all the people of my life. All my family, my friends, my acquaintances, and the suggestion also of all the people I am destined to meet in my future. A party is going on, with entertainment. Above us is a large, brilliant chandelier. In the far corner, to the left, is a big piano.

> The entertainment is provided by two figures near the piano. They appear to be North African shaykhs or marabouts; they are dressed in white jellabahs; each has a white turban or burnoose which covers the head and is wrapped around the neck beneath the chin. Their faces are black.

> The entertainment has to do with an animal which, in the dream, I think of as a "horse," though clearly it is a one-humped camel, a dromedary. The marabouts, who are armed with rifles, kill the camel, who then comes back to life. That's the entertainment. Anyone among the guests can request that the camel die in a certain way, after which it will again come back to life. I request, the next time they kill the camel, that it die with its legs buckling under it so that it twists to the left as it falls. I demonstrate this kind of death myself so that the marabouts will understand what I want, twisting to the left as I fall and making a "blaaaugh!" sound, like a camel,

then standing up again. They proceed to shoot the camel so that it dies exactly as I have demonstrated. Then it comes back to life, and stands up.

To the left of the large, red-papered cubical room is a doorway, which is reached by ascending perhaps two short steps. Beyond the doorway is a small, narrow room with plush, green-upholstered chairs, and a table upon which is a lamp with a yellow-green shade with yellow polkadots. Beyond this room is a darkened area of shabby, abandoned-looking halls with cracked and flaking plaster. The other two rooms are in vivid color, but this rear area is all in black-and-white. I enter the narrow room and pass into the rear area, then I return to the cubical room. I leave the cubical room and re-enter it for a second time, in exactly the same way. Then I leave it for a third time—but when I return for the third time to the cubical room, it is now pitch black, silent. Everyone is gone. I am alone.

At this point the dream become "lucid"; within the dream, I realize that I am dreaming. In my fear of abandonment I cry out to my mother and father, who I realize are sleeping in the next room—in terms of this world. I want them to awaken me from this dream which has ended in such a frightening way. They hear my cries, and do in fact awaken me.

> It is madness to cross the ocean
> Looking for the ocean itself,
> Madness to find a direction
> That doesn't appear
> On either globe or compass,
> And then turn toward it deliberately;
> Such things are not done.

God cannot be reached or accessed; the practice, rather, is to recognize His Presence in all entities, in all states, in all moments; they are His Self-revelations, not the products of our "research". To try to encompass the Essence of God produces madness—but madness is also a symbol of the *gnosis* that transcends the rational mind, what Omar Khayyam calls "a blind understanding".

> But when night comes, and the wind drops
> And the calm ocean reflects
> The mazes of the stars,
> Why not leave cloak of your existence

On the deck of the ship,
And dive, in your madness,
Into the glossy black water
That has carried you for fifty years
On the strict count of your breath,
And reach the Midnight Sun?

When the wind of mental passion subsides, the soul is unveiled as pure Substance; she becomes the perfect Mirror of God's thoughts. The ship is the Path—the Path, however, is not *to* God, but *in* God. As St. John of the Cross said, "If the motion of going were to continue forever, one would never arrive"; as Lew Welch said, "Trails go nowhere. / They end exactly / where you stop." Drowning is a Sufi symbol of Union; the Midnight Sun is *'illa 'Llah* within *La illaha*, the subsistence of the Absolute within the annihilation of the relative; the descent of the Waking state into the state of Deep Sleep.

When I was a man, I had no Self but God;
Now I am the Self of every woman and every man,
One with all who walk the path of Nothing.
All those who have become Nothing before they die
Have no Self but I. I am the road the stars travel
Before the face of their Lord.

The Arabic root TRQ refracts itself into various words meaning *path*; *road*; *spiritual Way*; *one who knocks* (as a metaphor for *night visitor*), and *path or orbit for the passage of stars or other heavenly bodies* (who are also "night visitors"). Jesus (speaking in Aramaic, closely allied to Arabic) called himself "the *Way*", and said: "Behold, I stand at the door and *knock*". And in Luke, Chap. 11, He tells the parable of the man, a night visitor, who knocks on his friend's door at midnight asking for bread to feed his guest, and says "*knock* and it shall be opened unto you."

I am a ladder seen in a dream;
Angels ascend and descend upon me; [Genesis 28:12]
My flesh is a highway of living intelligence.
When the seven seas rise like sap

[166]

Through the bark of the olive, changed into liquid light,
There I will stand, in neither the east nor the west. [Qur'an
 24:35]
When God summons the four winds back to His chamber,
Calling them each by its name,
I will be the body of that vast, returning sigh.

In Hindu terms, this is the voice of the *jivanmukhta*, the one who has
reached *moksha* in this very life. In Buddhist terms, this is the voice of
the Buddha who spontaneously lends his name and form as vehicles for
the Enlightenment of others, the Bodhisattva Vow being not a choice but
an intrinsic aspect of Buddhahood; if the Buddha still exists after
Enlightenment, it is only in service to and on behalf of those who still
believe in their own separate existence. In specifically Islamic terms, this
is the voice of *Imam al-Qaim al-Mahdi*.

To visit God is to spend the night inside the Sun,
The Sun who hears and sees, without sleep.

According to 'Abd al-Karim al-Jili, the seat of the Immortal Prophet
Khidr, patron of the Sufis, is in the realm of the Midnight Sun in the far
north; this, again, represents waking consciousness as mysteriously resi-
dent in the depths of Sleep—*a blind understanding*.

So shed the world, and open the gates of dawn:
The Sun is about to rise for the last time,
Climbing the green balconies of Axis Mundi, the luminous steps,
Gathering in the fruit of what has been,
Storing away the seeds of what shall be,
Till it stands on the floor of high eternity, the Temple Mount
And prostrates itself before the throne
Of the Light which does not set.

Here the Sun as the source of cosmic light is revealed as no more than
the servant of the Metacosmic Light (cf. Q. 6:76–80, where Abraham
worships first a star, then the Moon, then the Sun, until he sees that all of
them finally set, after which he worships Allah alone). The Sun here is a

symbol of the created intellect, the portal of cosmic manifestation—who, at the end of time, harvests and gathers up all the knowledge that constitutes universal manifestation (Q. 30:8: *Allah created not the heavens and the earth, and that which is between them, save with truth*) and presents it as a gift and a sacrifice to the Uncreated Intellect, at the very geographical point, on the very rock, where Abraham was prepared to sacrifice his son. It stores away in the "barns of God" the all the seeds of the next cycle-of-manifestation. And the golden cupola of the Dome of the Rock itself symbolizes the Uncreated Intellect, "*the Light which does not set*".

PART FOUR:
Lew Welch as Teacher

Lew Welch was both my poetic mentor and my first real teacher. But since he was also an alcoholic suicide, it was inevitable that I would have to separate his teaching into negative and positive aspects, the first to be rejected, the second to be accepted with gratitude. Part One of this essay has to do with the first kind of teaching, Part Two with the second.

I: BUZZARD CULT, ADIEU

My initiator into the art of poetry was Lew Welch. I learned many things of value from him, including some real metaphysical insights that I will deal with below, but his best lesson was negative: "Kid, don't end up like me."

In an attempt to "initiate" me, Lew introduced me to two people who had everything to do with my future spiritual development: Samuel Lewis ("Sufi Sam"), and Carlos Castaneda. Sufi Sam, a kind of bridge figure between the hippies and the world of real Sufi initiation, foreshadowed my entrance into the path of *tasawwuf*, while Castaneda was a lurid omen of my future magic-dabbling, and my lifelong oversensitivity to dark psychic forces.

Lew, like many poets of the Beat/Hippy era, sometimes thought of himself as a magician—and undoubtedly his most successful magic act was to conjure up a posthumous cult for himself, so as to mystify and glamourize what was, after all, just one more sordid alcoholic suicide.

He did this through a poem entitled *Song of the Turkey Buzzard*, which was his suicide note. In an attempt to invent something on the order of "American *koans*," Lew had composed three riddles: *The Riddle of Bowing*, *The Riddle of Hands*, and *The Rider Riddle*. *The Rider Riddle*, which is basically a way of finding one's helping spirit in the form of a "totem" animal or plant, goes like this:

> If you spend as much time on the Mountain as you
> should, she will always give you a Sentient Being to ride:
> animal, plant, insect, reptile, or any of the Numberless Forms:

> What do *you* ride?

> (There is one right answer for every person, and only
> that person can really know what it is.)

"The Mountain" is Mt. Tamalpais in Marin County, California. Lew asked this riddle of himself, and got "turkey buzzard" for an answer. In *Song of the Turkey Buzzard*, he says:

> The rider riddle is easy to ask
> But the answer might surprise you.
>
> How desperately I wanted Cougar
> (I, Leo, etc.)
> brilliant proofs: terrain,
> color, food, all
> nonsense. All made up.
>
> > *They were always there, the*
> > *laziest high-fliers, bronze-winged,*
> > *the silent ones.*
>
> . . . .
>
> They smell sweet
>   meat is dry on their talons
>
> The very opposite of
>   death
>
> bird of re-birth
>   buzzard
>
> meat is rotten meat made
>   sweet again....
>   . . . .
>
> > Hear my last Will & Testament:
>
> Among my friends there shall always be
> one with proper instructions
> for my continuance.

Let no one grieve.
I shall have used it all up
used up every bit of it.
What an extravagance!
What a relief!

On a marked rock, following his orders,
place my meat.

All care must be taken not to
frighten the natives of this
barbarous land, who
will not let us die, even
as we wish.

With proper ceremony disembowel what I
no longer need, that it might more quickly
rot and tempt

my new form

So the buzzards will eat Lew's guts and that's how he will be "reincarnated" as a Buzzard God. No personal immortality, not even any "spiritual" reincarnation, and certainly no *moksha*, no Perfect Total Enlightenment. Lew meat will become buzzard meat, and that's that. And note the flattering, wily come-on to his "successor": The *one* with proper instructions for the continuance of Lewis Barrett Welch is — why *me*, of course!

Never once (though Buzzard was Milarepa's totem bird) did I hear a word from Lew about Nirvana, the Dharmakaya, God, the Great Spirit, Brahman, the Tao, Allah, the Atman, or any other rendition of Absolute Truth. Like others of his generation he was interested in a kind of secularized, "tricksterish" Buddhism — the "Beat Zen" of Alan Watts — but hardly a word about Nirvana or Perfect Total Enlightenment as a state of Liberation in Absolute Reality. Well, maybe there are too many words on that subject already, too many words and not enough practice. But it's also possible that Lew basically shared Gary Snyder's view of Buddhism, which I heard from him on the occasion of Philip Whalen's memorial service at Green Gulch Zen Center: "Face it, Charles—Buddhism is *atheism.*"

The only moment of simple religious piety—that all-important Step One—in all of Lew's poetry is the following, entitled *He Asks for Guidance*:

> Avalokiteshvara, Buddha of Compassion, Original
> Bodhisattva, Who spoke the Prajñaparamita Sutra
>   of the heart,
> Kannon in Japan, Kuan-Yin in China, Chenrezig in
>   Tibet, no God, but guide, O
> countless thousands of returning men and women
> of every place and time,
> as Virgil for Dante, through Dante's Hell,
> please guide me through Samsara.

Lew might have known more than he said; he certainly *was* more than he said, as we all are—but note this: It's not "please *liberate* me from Samsara," but "please *guide me through* Samsara." Well, in a way that's a modest, honest request, a realistically muted expectation. But if Avalokiteshvara is not a living symbol of Absolute Reality in the guise of Perfect Total Enlightenment—and in Lew's rendition of him, we are not really sure he is—then whence his power to guide? And if Lew could not believe in Absolute Reality, then how could be become available to that guidance? It was Beatrice who sent Virgil, and St. Lucy who sent Beatrice, and the Blessed Virgin who sent St. Lucy, and the Will of God working through the Blessed Virgin. But who or what sent Lew's Avalokiteshvara? Alavokiteshvara is the emanation of the Dharmakaya, the Original Mind, the Clear Light of the Void. Lew Welch's grasp on this truth, however, was unsteady. After Hell comes the *Purgatorio*, and the *Paradiso* after that; would that Lew could have seen, and named, the whole Path that stretched before him.

Lew Welch was in many ways a materialist. He usually scorned Christianity: "Who could ever worship a *Holy Ghost?*"—though he once said to me (I was basically in my Blakean Christian period then), "Maybe Jesus really is your Master." And it was this materialistic nature-worhip—essentially the "paganism" of Sir James Frazer and Robert Graves (the two books he told me every poet should read were *The*

Golden Bough and *The White Goddess*)—that replaced for him any kind of, effective, serious Buddhism, which would have started him out with certain basic behavioral requirements, like "no booze." And so he fell back, at least partly, on a simple, literal worship of the earth and sun:

> Here comes the sun. It's the only god we've got. It's shining on the earth. It [the earth] is our mother. It is a big round ball [from *How I Work as a Poet*].

So how does a materialist conceive of immortality—apart, that is, from the ministrations of cryogenics and genetic engineering? Lew's way was to opt for what is called "poetic immortality," which is essentially *immortality in the memory of the living*. But he went a step further. I believe that Lew Welch also wanted to be *held in a stable form and a conscious state after death* by that same memory. That's why he founded his Buzzard Cult. He wanted to trap and hold the attention of others after his death so as to maintain his identity—something he undoubtedly also did during life. When the Mexicans, on the Day of the Dead, put tortillas and tequila on the graves of the departed, they are doing the same thing. They are trying to keep the dead "alive" as ghosts—well-fed ghosts who will hopefully be satisfied enough not to vampirize the living. Lew, however, may ultimately have been unable to avoid the vampire trip, as witness at least two copycat suicides I certainly know of, those of Jack Boyce—an "accidental" death that was undoubtedly suicidal in intent— and "Burl," a sleepy, sodden youth who attached himself to Lew's wife Magda after Lew disappeared. But what is kept "alive" by the psychic energy of the living is not the actual spirit of the departed, but only the ghostly residue of the unredeemed psyche—in other words, the *ego:* the original vampire. In the words of W. B. Yeats, from *All Souls' Night*, Lew ultimately wanted to be one who had

> ....a ghost's right
> His element is so fine
> Being sharpened by his death
> To drink from the wine-breath
> While our gross palates drink from the whole wine.

That *is* a pretty classy-sounding afterlife—until you actually get there and see what it's like. The narcissist sacrifices his living flesh and spirit to the vampire of his self-image. "We invent ourselves," wrote Lew in *The Entire Sermon by the Red Monk*, "out of ingredients we didn't choose, by a process we can't control…. All you really say [supreme irony!] is 'Love me for myself alone'…. It is also possible to *uninvent* yourself. By a process you can't control. But you invented Leo. Forget it." Lew, in this poem, defines his poetic persona, "Leo," as the product of a *successful* act of narcissism—as if there could be such a thing—and explicitly rejects the spiritual Path: *the path of self-uninvention*. But no act of narcissism can really be "successful," simply because narcissism is a living hell. Gleaming in the reflected light of your own radiant image in the pool, you trap and lock the attention of everyone around you. But none of that attention really *gets* to you. All the love and admiration and compassion and help you so desperately (and silently) crave is attracted to and eaten by that endlessly talking image, leaving the real you starving: this is the *oral hell* the Buddhists reserve for those they call the *pretas*, the "hungry ghosts." Lew was capable of making many people love him, but could receive love from no-one. He let himself starve all his life for the love that might have saved him, because it would have destroyed his glorious self-image, his "Leo." He even claimed to have made the youngest suicide-attempt on record, by going on a hunger-strike while still on the bottle—and (ironically) the bottle was the one thing he never got off of. Lew had so deeply despaired of the love he needed that he was finally willing to sacrifice himself to the self-image he *thought* was actually getting it—and if he had to live through a quasi-eternity as a Buzzard God, he figured that was a small price to pay for *the food*. An image on a TV screen cannot receive love, however, and all who give their love to such subhuman images are signing up for an extended stay in *Xbalbá*, the Castle of the Vampires.

And the saddest thing is, so many of us (including myself) "bought" the Buzzard Cult. Whenever we'd see a turkey buzzard sail over, we'd say, "there goes Lew." The Buzzard Cult allowed us to deny *everything*: that Lew, by his suicide, had demonstrated at least some pretty serious flaws in his spiritual life; that all those glamorous bohemian death-trips were nothing but simple despair after all; that we too needed love, and to give love, but had despaired of ever finding it, given up on it so long ago we couldn't even remember it, despite all the counterculture propaganda of the Beatles and so many others, their wan, pastel mewing about "love is all you need." (It wasn't love we were singing about, it was only sex...and ultimately it wasn't even sex we were singing about, it was only pornography, only *images*—"sexual" or "spiritual" as you will.) Lew trained us to seek inflated glamour instead of true love—love, of course, being "romantic," "unhip," something requiring some level of basic humility, some modicum of genuine, sincere, unglamorous humanity. How Philistine! How bourgeois! How beneath the Pride of the Lion! And how bleak and terrible the forboding, in the craw of the glamour-addict, of the withdrawal to come, the terminal deadness of reality without all that psychic glamour to keep it hopping. (To endure that deadness, that "dry drunk," without looking away, like "the salt of the earth," is the sole key to the renewal of life—that, and a basic faith in God, an understanding that Reality, in Lew's words, "goes on whether I look at it or not." In Shakespeare's *The Merchant of Venice*, the portrait of Portia is found in the leaden casket, not in the gold or silver ones. Only lead—found, accepted, and lived with—can be transmuted into the Alchemical Gold.)

In his *Axe Handles*, Gary Snyder has a poem entitled *For/From Lew*:

> Lew Welch just turned up one day,
> Live as you and me. "Damn, Lew" I said,
> "you didn't shoot yourself after all."
> "Yes I did" he said,
> and even then I felt the tingling down my back.
> "Yes you did, too—I can feel it now."
> "Yeah," he said,
> "There's a basic fear between your world and
> mine. I don't know why.
> What I came to say, was,
> Teach the children about the cycles.
> The life cycles. All the other cycles.
> That's what it's all about, and it's all forgot."

I've always had the impression that this poem must have been based on a dream that Gary had. Around the time it was probably written, and certainly before I read it, I also had a dream about Lew, which resulted in the following poem; the last four lines of it were dictated, word for word, in the dream itself:

I saw the Sun set up in the distance, like a temple on a plain
Animals crashing through forests inside its face.
And my dead teacher, seated, on the orbit of the Earth,
Musing on his old love the Earth and Sun,
And allowing himself, sadly,
To forget it.

This is the age when all stories have been told
The dead going on without poetry,
And poetry telling them the
Truth of gravity's art.

I believe that these two poems are parts of the same "message" from Lew. For him to be sitting on the orbit of the earth in my dream is also a reference to "cycles," but with a different twist—more like the Buddhist "wheel of existence" that the Buddhas no longer turn on because they are now sitting at the center of it, "the still point of the turning world" (T. S. Eliot from *The Four Quartets*).

In another vision I had of Lew after his death, he said to me: "Things don't change here as fast as I thought they would." This is the wages of the Buzzard Cult. He thought our attention to him after his death would save him, but all it did (maybe, maybe) was imprison him. If so, we'd better do what we can to turn him loose—and holding on to a false, idealistic memory of a "great teacher" when we should be praying for the liberation of a despairing soul in torment is definitely not the way to do it. Lew *was* a great teacher in many ways—but if we're ever going to *matriculate*, we will have to confront his last, and toughest, lesson.

So I hereby declare the Buzzard Cult officially dissolved, before everybody who ever heard of it passes from this world. It was a kind of drug, designed by Lew and all the rest of us, to sedate us against the unbearable tragedy of those times. When it comes to the turkey buzzard drug, I for one am going cold turkey.

II: FREEDOM FROM THE WORLD OF WORDS

It is common to hear people say things like: "Poetry (or whatever other art) is my spiritual Path." However, people like Plato, or Ramana Maharshi, or Muhammad, or Jalaluddin Rumi, who actually functioned as guides on the spiritual Path, were extremely wary of poetry. Plato, in the *Republic*, called poets "liars"; Ramana Maharshi discouraged the composition of poetry because it diverts spiritual potential away from Liberation and toward self-expression; and the Prophet Muhammad (peace and blessings be upon him), in the *surah* of the Qur'an called "The Poets", heard straight from God that poets can best be described as those who *say that which they do not*. And Rumi called poetry "tripe." Be that as it may, can poetry still be a spiritual Path in some way, or at least part of one?

The basic problem with poetry, in spiritual terms, is that it falsely suggests to us that a poet is a *creator*, that the world called into being by the poetic art is in some sense a real world. But the truth is, only God creates. To believe anything else, to believe that the human being as poet, or as technologist, or as political leader is in some sense a co-creator in partnership with God, is heresy, and blasphemy—by which I mean that it is simply not true. Everything has already been created by God, from all eternity; man, apart from God, can create nothing. The ego, however, will not accept this. It begins by seeing itself as a co-creator with God, and ends by taking itself to *be* God. Instead of understanding all things as words spoken by God, first in eternity and then in time, it forgets that it has first *heard* these words, and only later learned how to speak them. It forgets that "In the beginning was the word, and the word was with God, and the word was God." Thus we can say that the deluded poet is the very image of the ego's foolish self-deification, and all the disastrous consequences that go with it.

Still, whether we are poets or not, we are now fallen—fallen into the world of words. We do not see reality; we do not live in a real world. We inhabit a phoney world "created" by our obsessive, unconscious, verbal definitions of things, the kingdom of the monkey-mind. And given that this false, delusive, beguiling and terrifying world is produced by our *unconsciousness* of the effects of human language on our perception of things, only a complete *consciousness* of those effects can free us from that world, that *samsara*; like William Burroughs once said, "Communication must be made conscious and total: that's the only way to stop it." And who, at least in potential, are more conscious of the effects and qualities of human language than the poets? Nonetheless, we will never become conscious enough of what human language is and how it operates on us simply by *talking*; we also need to learn, in the words of Lew Welch from his poem *Wobbly Rock*, how "to sit real still and keep your mouth shut." (Wobbly Rock, as Lew says in the poem itself, is "a real rock... resting on actual sand at the surf's edge:/ Muir Beach, California.... Size of the largest haystack/It moves when hit by waves/Actually shudders." Lew used to sit on that rock to meditate; it has a precisely square little step or cleft on it that makes a perfect meditation seat [half lotus]. I've meditated there myself.)

The Provençal words *trouvère* and *troubadour* mean "finder"; the Greek word *poetes* means "maker." If we think that we, as speakers, are makers first and finders only second, we are deluded. Only God is the First Speaker; we are *finders* first, finders of the First Words of God spoken in Eternity; only later are we makers. We work exclusively on what has already been given, and—if we are true makers, not chaotic babblers—only *according* to what has already been given. If we want to take the audacious and dangerous step of speaking human words, we will have to learn how to *listen* first—and to hear is to obey.

⊕

One thing Lew Welch tried to teach was how to squeeze many meanings into a few words, a skill which is related to the opposite, *hermeneutic* ability to unpack those meanings, to unfold them, expand them, bring them to light. This reciprocity between synthesis and analysis, between composition and exegesis, puts us in touch with the alternation of the seasons, with the birth and death of animals and human beings, and ultimately with the creation and destruction of the universe. It teaches us that God is always and hiding from us in the act of showing Himself, and showing Himself in the act of hiding from us; He is always creating the universe by composing it, and then destroying it by revealing the inner meaning of what was composed. As Lew said, posthumously, in Gary Snyder's poem *For/From Lew*: "Teach the children about the cycles/ The life cycles, all the other cycles./ That's what it's all about, and it's all forgot."

Lew's deepest and densest attempt to pack the most lore into the fewest words is his poem *Doctor, Can You Spell Nebuchadnezzar Without Any Z?** (*Overheard from the mouth of a senile old Irish lady on her deathbed.):

[179]

A turf and a clod spells "Nebuchad"

A knife and a razor spells "Nebuchadnezzar"

Two silver spoons and a gold ring
Spells Nebuchadnezzar, the King.

My first impression of this poem was, "Nice, extremely pleasurable, it has density, it's tasty, I can chew it. But it's slight, it's just word-play, it's only melody." Somehow, though, it unconsciously engaged my understanding, till I came up with a deeper interpretation: *A turf and a clod*: The grave. *A knife and a razor:* Surgery (razor to shave the skin, scalpel to cut it). *Two silver spoons and a gold ring:* A hard marriage, two doted-on children, all finally wearing her out. The title: Two ideas of death intersecting in delirium—the last letter of the alphabet representing death, and Nebuchadnezzar as King Death, to whom she is espoused. She asks the doctor if she can escape death by a spell, or re-spelling, of her fate. The poem's answer is: "No". And note how time flows backwards: Death, surgery, childbirth, marriage. This is what the Tibetans call "the *bardo* of seeking rebirth." In the words of Eliot, from *The Wasteland*: "He passed the stages of his age and youth/ entering the whirlpool" (*samsara*).

But Lew's more central teaching, one that was more in line with his *perceptual* Buddhism, was all about how to become free of the world of words, free from one's own subjectivity; in other words, how to reach objective consciousness. In *"Everybody Calls Me Tricky, But My Real Name's Mr. Earl": A Sermon*, he says:

Those who live in the words of words kill us who seek
Union with
What goes on whether we look at it or not

The teaching given in these lines has two parts to it: That there really is a real world that goes on whether we look at it or not, that it's not all just "in your head"; and that it's important to become consciously one with that world, not just believe in it. The "world of words" is a nice place to visit, though you wouldn't want to live there; yet words were Lew Welch's stock in trade. Given that, as Lew says of "the true rebel" in the same poem, *"And yet he must speak!"*, how can we deal with words so that they will help unite us with, not separate us from, what goes on whether we look at it or not? In order to answer this, I need to take a short philosophical detour. (As Lew once said to me, "You have an almost pathological belief in the reality of ideas". I would answer him, now, by saying: "True! There were times when those moths almost ate me to the bone. But you had an almost pathological disbelief in the reality of them because you followed William Carlos Williams' idea of 'no ideas but in things', as if Aristotle could father poets, but not Plato. Why don't you ask Yeats how true that is, if you ever get a chance to talk with him?")

The Scholastic Realists (mostly following Plato) said that categories of things are real, which is why we can discern them; all individuals in a given category share a common essence, and that essence is realer than the individuals who make it up. The Scholastic Nominalists (like William of Occam) said that categories of things are conventional, not real; they are arbitrarily conjured up by words alone; the individuals within them share no real common essence.

Realism is intrinsic to the metaphysical worldview, which is inseparable from the notion that levels of being are real, and that higher levels of being are realer than lower ones. It is also the basis of the idea that individual have *souls*, a "soul" being defined as "a higher level of being resident within a lower one, and expressing itself by means of the lower one." Consequently, most religious worldviews are basically realist.

Nominalism is one of the origins of postmodern nihilism. If only individuals exist, if essences such as "humanity" are unreal, if they are mere names, then to consider a human individual to be in any sense a *person* is unwarranted. And if only individuals are real, then a human being's body must be realer than his soul, his cells realer than his body, the molecules that make up his cells realer than those cells, etc.; corporeal, psychological or spiritual integrity—*unity* of any kind—is an illusion. It's obvious that no essentially religious or spiritual view of things can exist within a Nominalist mindset.

But Realism also has a negative side, spiritually speaking: the *idolatry of abstraction*, the negation of particular individuals in the name of the category they occupy, the false idea that categories, considered to be realer than individuals, are at the same time abstractions drawn *from* individuals rather than higher and more comprehensive levels of individuality itself—concrete living beings who contain, in synthetic mode, all the qualities of all the individuals who share their essence. (William Blake, in his figure of Urizen, god of tyrannical abstraction, and his doctrine of "minute particulars", attacks this kind of idolatry.) In other words, to say—in the name of Realism—that abstraction is realer than individuality is actually to take a step toward Nominalism. To "abstract" is to discern a common quality in a set of particulars; and if abstract categories are drawn from particulars, not the other way around, then—as the Nominalists claim—those particulars must be realer than their category.

Nominalism, however, also has a spiritually positive side: the potential of demonstrating that the world is real beyond our definitions of it, that if we can free ourselves from the abstract categories in terms of which we experience things—categories that are based mostly on language, and unconscious language at that—then we will see things as they really are.

The Buddhists say: "To name a thing is to kill it", to imprison it inside a lifeless abstraction. Some schools of Hindu thought, in line with the worldviews of most archaic or religiously-based societies, say: "The name of a thing is an intrinsic part of it". According to this theory, to name something is to make it actually present: to name beings is to *summon* them, to *call* them by their name. To ask "what, or by what name, are you called?" is to ask "By what word are you summoned? By what name are you made present?" So the Buddhists, who teach that "all things are without self-nature", have certain affinities with the Nominalists—except that they believe that not only categories but individuals too are unreal (in a sense)—while those who believe that the names of things are real parts of those things are closer to the Realists: only real things can have real names. If the names of things were not intrinsic aspects of them, it would not be possible to assert, as many spiritual traditions do, that "God and His Name are One"; consequently the *dhikr* of the Sufis, the *mnimi Theou* of the Eastern Orthodox Christians, and the *japa-yoga* of the Hindus would be invalid. Nor, in terms of Catholic doctrine, would the Transubstantiation by an ordained priest of simple unleavened wheat bread into the Body of Christ be possible by virtue of the words *Hoc est enim Corpus Meum*. On the other hand, the traditions that assert the "realism of names" also teach that God is absolutely beyond name and form, as in the Hindu practice designated by the words *neti, neti*—"not this, not that"—as well as in such writings as the *Mystical Theology* of Dionysius the Areopagite, that reads just like a Mahayana *sutra*. But if the Buddhists did not also hold in some fashion to the doctrine that "a thing and its name are one," the use of *mantras* would not form so important a part of Mahayana and Vajrayana practice, since *mantras* summon the effective reality of the insight or energy or state of consciousness they designate.

That's the *theory*, but what about the *practice*? What is the practical use of the doctrine that "to name something is to kill it", and of the seemingly opposite doctrine that "the name of a thing is an intrinsic part of it"?

The practical use of both doctrines is to free us from the world of words. If we realize that our experience of the world is obscured and conditioned by the verbal definitions we impose upon it, and that those definitions are largely carried by obsessive, unconscious, sub-vocal speech, then we will also realize that to become silent within is to see all things as they really are. So our way is clear.

On the other hand, to understand how the name of something is an intrinsic part of it is to *objectify language*, to get words out of our heads and into the world around us. It is to free language from the grasp of the ego—the little, unconscious self-identified self that thinks it can call a thing anything it wants to because it *owns language*, because it, not God, is the Creator of the Universe. And once the ego releases its grip on language, it dissolves, because the ego is mostly the product of language—of the human identification with, and internalization of, the world around it, by means of language fallen from the level of conscious *summoning* to the level of habitual unconscious chatter. If we could name things so consciously and so deliberately that we could actually command their presence—if we could remain in perfect silence until a word of power is born in us, a word that suddenly bursts out of us to unite with its object like an arrow to the bull's-eye—unconscious sub-vocal speech would be destroyed: this, precisely, is the *tantric* use of human speech. And in order to speak in this way, we will need to understand exactly how, in Lew's words, "To become enamored of our powers is to lose them, at once!", and solve the dilemma he expressed as "How can I learn to get out of my way?" When our speech becomes so powerful, when it rises from so deep a silence, that it can actually command the presence of the thing being named, then *we* are no longer speaking; no one is speaking, in a state like this, but God Himself.

So perfect silence and perfectly conscious speech ultimately come down to the same thing, spiritually speaking. In meditation we learn that we cannot silence our internal dialogue without listening to it, and that we cannot listen to it unless we are silent. Only in the act of listening can the separation of speech and silence be overcome. Listening, because it annihilates us as speakers, makes words objective to us; they are no longer unconsciously jabbering on inside our heads. Even if we hear them with our inner ear, they are still part of the world around us, like the sound of the traffic or the songs of birds. And if our own internal speech is now outside of us, we are no longer identified with the verbal mind; we are now sitting behind that mind, silently listening to it. And as we listen to it, we simultaneously understand that it is not outside us at all, any more than it is inside us. It is one with us—and as for us, we are not there at all. It is one with us *because* we are not there at all. The verbal mind is all we used to be; now that we no longer *are* it, we no longer *are*. And if we no longer are—then there we are. (This is the Buddhist teaching of *shunyata* and *tathata*, the Sufi teaching of *fana* and *baqa*).

This kind of freedom from the verbal mind and the world it invents is what the Zen *koans* are designed to produce. Two of the three "riddles" Lew composed—*The Riddle of Bowing* and *The Riddle of Hands*—are also designed to set us free from the world of words. Lew said of them: "They are Koans for beginners, making no claim for Perfect Enlightenment, but those who solve them will discover a deep spiritual insight." Here they are:

THE RIDDLE OF BOWING

In every culture, in every place and time, there has always been a religion, and in every one of these religions there has always been the gesture of bowing so fully that the forehead strikes the ground.

Why is this?
(There is only one right answer to this riddle)

THE RIDDLE OF HANDS

In every culture, in every place and time, there has always been a religion, and in every one of these religions there has always been the gesture of hands clasped together, as Christians do to pray.

Why is this?

(There is only one right answer to this riddle)

I must now declare that I am empowered to say "pass" or "fail" to anyone who wants to tackle these riddles, because Lew told me the answer to *Bowing* and I solved *Hands* by myself; my solution was later confirmed by Magda Cregg. All I can say by way of a clue is that the answers to these riddles are entirely concrete, completely beyond the world of words, though not (like the true Zen *koans*) totally beyond the world of form. Each one has only one right answer. I can't reveal the answers to these riddles because I was entrusted with them, but I can give you the answer to another riddle, the one that appears in *Wobbly Rock*:

> *Dychymig Dychymig:* (riddle me a riddle)

> Waves and the sea. If you
> take away the sea

> Tell me what it is

The answer is: If you take away "the sea" from "Waves and the sea," you get "Waves and," which, to the ear, is also "wave-sand". So the solution is something anyone who has seen a sandy ocean beach has seen: the pattern of waves, or ripples, left by the ebbing tide in the drying sand.

This stationary wave-pattern is *tathata*, "suchness"; the absent sea is *shunyata*, "voidness". *Shunyata* is analogous to the Aristotelian concept of *being*: that by virtue of which a thing simply is, without regard to its name or form. *Tathata* is analogous to the Aristotelian *essence*: That by virtue of which a thing is what it is, is this but not that, whether or not it actually exists. To separate *shunyata* from *tathata*, Being from Essence— to separate the sea from the waves—and then reunite them on a higher level, is what all true art does, to break us free from our habitual ways of looking at things and "cleanse the doors of perception". If we believe that things are heavy literal lumps then we can safely ignore them (we say to ourselves). But if we understand them as *apparitions*, if we see them precisely as "things seen", then we have nowhere to hide from them, and they, no way to hide from us. The Chinese landscape painter, say of the Sung period, renders his pine branches, waterfalls and misty crags simply by removing the *literal being* of his subject, and leaving only the essence, the "suchness" of it (though not, of course, the being of the painting; the Essence of his subject, first given being by water, timber, rock and air, is now made to Be by ink and rice paper). And when the essence or *suchness* of, say, a landscape is separated from its *being*, in the literal sense of that word—separated, in other words, from the unconscious conviction that "of course the landscape *exists*, that goes without saying; so what else is new?"—then the suchness of it can appear purely as *void*, and that voidness be revealed as its true *being*. The great classical Chinese or Japanese painter does not try to *reproduce* nature, like the "realistic" or "naturalistic" artist, but rather makes a painting which, because it is obviously an "apparition," an image, and not an imitation or counterfeit of a real thing, thereby reveals the essence of its subject—so that, when we find ourselves walking through a landscape of pine trees and waterfalls and misty crags, and suddenly recall such an image, it immediately superimposes itself upon and blends with the picture painted by our senses, since there is no "rivalry of two beings" to prevent it. And so we suddenly witness a world in which essence fully reveals being, a world where, in Lew's words, "things *are* exactly what they *seem*."

This riddle has the virtue, unlike *The Riddle of Hands* and *The Riddle of Bowing* of also being a pun: "waves and/ waves sand". Puns were very important to Lew Welch; I could never understand why until now. His puns were not particularly funny, nor were they meant to be—like the last line of *Hiking Poem/High Sierra*, "you bear with me." To "bear with" someone is to put up with them, but Lew is also saying that the reader bears the same burden that he does, the burden of being human, a job that sometimes gets to be a real *bear* (not to mention the fact that, in the high Sierras, one might well encounter a bear for real). And once, when as a high school student I showed him an early poem with the word "groove" in it (in the colloquial Beat/hippy usage), he responded by saying, "Don't you really mean *grove*?" That wasn't even a pun, it was only a near-pun. There wasn't anything witty about it, unless he was covertly pegging me as a Platonist, an "academic" (*academy*, the name of Plato's school, being from the Greek word for *grove*). But what was he up to? At least his puns in [*I Saw Myself*] and *Wobbly Rock* had some real poetic power behind them:

> I saw myself
> a ring of bone
> In the clear stream
> of all of it....
>
> And then heard
> "ring of bone" where
> ring is what a
> bell does

And:

> Rock
> Returning to the sea, easily, as
> Sea once rose from it. It
> Is a sea rock
>
> (easily)
>
> I am
> Rocked by the sea

To be "rocked by the sea" is to be seated, next to the sea and surrounded by it, on a rock that rocks. But why bother incorporating such bathetic puns into poems that seem to be doing quite well without them? It's kind of ingenious; it's sort of cute; it's even rather striking in a way that's hard to describe or account for—but what, if anything, is it *for*?

[187]

What it's for is to free the reader from the world of words. Usually, habitually, unconsciously, we identify things with their names. What is a rock? Why it's a *rock*, of course! That heavy solid object sitting there on the seashore is a *rock* and nothing else. What else could it be? But when the same word is presented to us as meaning two or more things at the same time—ring as a round hollow object and ring as a sound, bear as "to carry" and bear as an animal's name, rock as a natural object made of stone and rock as a back-and-forth motion—then the word is separated from its object. And when a word is separated from its object, it becomes an object in itself; it is now *objective* to the listening mind. (Once a word is separated from its object, then—if we so choose—it can be reunited with that object in order to reveal new things about it; "rock" as a seemingly solid object can now also be seen as something that "rocks" or vibrates back and forth, which is the actual quality of matter as revealed by modern physics, like the pattern of waves left in the sand—but that's not the level of meaning we are considering here.)

Lew worked hard at making language *opaque*—something he learned from Gertrude Stein. He said (in *How I Work as a Poet*), that "most people who call themselves poets don't realize that you can't make a poem out of anything except language—any more than a bricklayer can build a brick wall out of anything but bricks". But his language could also be transparent at the same time. The language of, say, Dylan Thomas in his poem *Altarwise by Owl-light*—"Altarwise by owl-light in the half-way house/ The gentleman lay graveward with his furies" etc. etc.—is opaque first because we can't figure out what it means (until later), but more particularly because the images it produces in our minds (its *phanopoeia*) are largely eaten up by its interesting musical language (its *melopoeia*). At the other extreme, the language of some Japanese *haiku* will tend to be completely transparent, its *phanopoeia* dominating and absorbing its *melopoeia*—like this one by Basho:

> A wild sea—
> In the distance
> Over Sado
> The Milky Way

But, at its best, Lew's linguistic opacity is at one with his linguistic transparency, as in this passage from *Wobbly Rock*:

Below us:
>> fronds of kelp
>> fish
>> crustaceans
>> eels

Then us
>> then rocks at the cliff's base
>> starfish
>> (hundreds of them sunning themselves)
>> final starfish on the highest rock then

Cliff
>> 4 feet up the cliff a flower
>> grass
>> further up more grass
>> grass over the cliff's edge
>> branch of pine then

Far up the sky

>> a hawk

The effect of this union of opacity and transparency is to make his language both concrete, like a plank or a brick, and also empty, like a doorway—a doorway through which we can see the world with various objects in it, among which are the very words Lew is using to describe it. This, along with the riddle, the pun, and various statements where he lets us in on what he's up to, is how Lew uses poetry to objectify language, and by so doing free us from the world of words. As he said to me once, "Only poets know that words don't mean anything." He could have meant this in the nihilistic, Nominalist sense that denies the reality of essences or qualities, viewing them as mere abstractions. More likely, however, he meant it in the more-or-less Zen sense, that words are not to be identified with the things they describe, but are to be seen as objects in their own right, like trees or rocks or birds. And if words are also objects, then it is also possible to see, in the Realist sense, that they are the resonant aspects of the very objects they signify—that if a hoot-owl says "hu" to our outer ears, there is also a way in which, to our inner ear, a rock is saying "rock". *We* don't name things; things name themselves *to* us. That's another way of understanding, in poetic mode, how "words don't mean anything."

[189]

Furthermore, Lew's teaching designed to free us from the world of words did not always use words exclusively. For example, the first time I met him, in a landscaped garden area at the College of Marin (I was there sitting in for my friend Bill Trumbly, who was too hung over to attend Lew's class; the only other student present was then Dominican nun, and both then and now poet, Mary Norbert Körte), he said: "Take a look at those trees over there. Now imagine the spaces between the trees as solid objects, and the trees themselves as empty spaces." And we did it; we saw as he saw. In so doing, we perceptually actualized (I realized later) the famous line "form is emptiness, emptiness is form" from the *Heart Sutra*, and learned how to see the world not as a set of literal objects—as our unconscious identification of things with our names for them had taught us to do—but rather as an *apparition*, as *maya*. As Lew said, "I try to write from the poise of mind that lets me see how things are exactly what they seem"—not how they *are what they are*, but how they *are what they seem*—in view of the fact that what they *are* is, precisely, a *seeming*. That perceptual seed Lew planted in my psyche—a little like those shamanic perception exercises designed to deconstruct the world in Carlos Castaneda's *Journey to Ixtlan*, though Lew taught me his own exercise way before Castaneda's first book *The Teachings of Don Juan* came out—sprouted years later, when, meditating with my eyes open in a redwood grove in Gerstle Park in San Rafael, California, the redwood grove was suddenly transformed into a birch grove: the redwoods, empty; the spaces between them, birch trees.

A deeper and more complete perception exercise—or at least the suggestion for one—appears in "Wobbly Rock":

> On a trail not far from here
> Walking in meditation
> We entered a dark grove
> And I lost all separation in step with the
> Eucalyptus as the train walked back beneath me

What exactly is happening here? The perceiver's sense of himself as an object walking through a Eucalyptus grove is replaced by the sense that the perceiver is motionless—except for his legs' stride—and that the Eucalyptus grove and the ground it rises from are moving backwards, past him and beneath him. This experience is analogous to that of the

Mevlevi or "whirling" dervishes when they practice their "turning" exercise. To begin with it seems to the dervish as if the environment were stationary and he turning counter-clockwise—but then a perceptual shift occurs: now the dervish is standing still, and the world is turning around him, clockwise; he has become "the still point of the turning world." (Interestingly, if the dervish stops turning before this shift occurs he will become dizzy, but if stops after the shift, no dizziness is experienced.)

The Buddhist take on such perceptual shifts, the dialectic of it, goes something like this: "We habitually base our sense of reality on our perception of things. But if this perception can be completely altered (by intoxicants, by yogic practices, or simply by turning our head to look in another direction), then it disappears as an absolute criterion for what is real. Consequently there is no way we can say for sure either that the perceiver is moving and the world is stationary, or that the world is moving and the perceiver is stationary. All we have are patterns of perception. These patterns cannot be called 'objective', since they can be altered at will by the subject, but neither can they be called 'subjective', since they include both subject and object, both perceiver and world, and the world is something that 'goes on whether we look at it or not'. Conclusion: the world and the one perceiving it are not *literally* real; they are empty apparitions arising in the One Mind". Lew's own rendition of this dialectic appears in his poem *Four Studies in Perception*; the setting is Golden Gate Park:

> A grove of Laurel grows in the city park.
> It grows whether I look at it or not,
> By a path deliberately unintended (unattended).
>
> I can find it. I can see it. I can sing:
>
> > *Magical Tree!*
> > *Leaf in my mother's stew!*
> > *Crown! Chew*
> > *Thy leaves to brighten*
> > *color in my eyes?*
>
> But all of it,

Singer, Song, the Grove itself
disappears, instantly,
if only I look another way.

If I only look another way, I make
Bulldozers, Baseball Players, and, later
Owls

There is also a Hindu explanation for the perceptual shift experienced by the whirling dervish or the meditative walker: "When the *atman* dawns—the Unseen Seer, the Absolute Witness who is the One Self of All—it is He who is motionless, and the Universe who moves. He is impassive, adamantine *Shiva*: She is powerful, dancing *Shakti*. He is the rock, but She does all the rocking".

⊕

Lew Welch's worldview, and his teaching, were based on three things: A personal myth that died with him (first "Leo" and then "Turkey Buzzard"); a more-or-less Neo-Pagan earth-worship that had some value for opening our eyes to the world around us, but that finally made it intolerable for Lew to live in a time of environmental degradation, since if there is no God Who is beyond this world as well as within it, if this world is all there is, then the decay of the earth is, effectively, the decay of Reality itself; and his own unique brand of perceptual Buddhism, which was a real contribution to the way of Perfect Total Enlightenment. May what was mortal in his teaching die forever; may what was immortal in his teaching enlighten us, and him.

PART FIVE:
Sufi Poems

I: The Ruins of the Feast

I

Ever since my skull was split by the stroke of the double axe, I have served two masters.

One says, "Do not pray—because you know me, you are already greater than any prostration, any *namaẓ*.

Follow no Prophet—because you serve me you are done with laws and finished with prophets."

The other says: "Take the hem of the robe of the Prophet Muhammad, hold on tight and never let go."

One night Eblis whispered to me: "Muhammad, a decent enough swineherd and certainly a skillful dog-trainer, is good enough for your soul, but your Heart is reserved for Someone greater.

Give your soul to the Law, if you must, but give your Heart to God alone."

But then, like lightning, I heard the voice of Another: "Your soul is not worthy of the Law; that's why it loves to fight with dogs and roll in the mud with pigs.

Only your Heart can withstand those commands and prohibitions, which are nothing other than the kisses and slaps of the Beloved from behind the veil.

Who tries to seize Me in the marketplace will never be invited to My House;

Who tries to break into My House through the window instead of entering by the door,

By the cowardly lust of the eye instead of the firm steps of a man, will become like a cloud of scattered moths in the declining day.

If you are a man, take that burning coal in your hand, and watch while the black rain-clouds of My Mercy gather in the East.

The bitter ocean of this world boils and smokes; the evening breeze brings news from the Garden

Paradise and the Fire are near.

The soul is like a swarm of flies over a rotting carcass, but the Law is the shape of a man; it stands erect.

And the Heart is the final Silence, ringing with My speech—the pure white page, unlettered, destitute,

That seeks no other word."

II

My eyes have served two masters, and divided my skull between them,
    but my heart has seen beyond the yea and the nay, beyond promise
        and betrayal.
If you take Islam away I will follow it hard, through seven barren
    valleys, into that black treasure cave where the ear of man first heard
        it, to which every loud and talkative thief
Has lost the map and the key.
If you take the Qur'an away I will become the Qur'an; I will take the
    Pen to my heart like a lance in battle; I will keep no knowledge of
        what is written in me.
And when you take yourself away, scornful of imitators, your fiery track
    across the sky, from which rose petals and musk and shards of
        splintered frankincense rain down to bewilder us, and blind us
            to your destiny,
Will be my burning road. You fade back, before the rocks, before the
    stars, before the drawn ranks of the ocean waves, before the word
        "Be!",
And I fade back with you. Behind the body's battlements. Behind the
    veil of the soul, whatever color, clear or clouded, may have dyed it.
        Through the door of the heart, fixed ajar in that one split second,
            now and forever. Up the steps of the wind, and behind it. Into
                the twelve-thousand facets of the Secret. Into the direction-
                less abyss where the Secret whispers Itself to Itself alone,
                and is lost in the Night of God.

You ruined the world only to attract me and capture me. You ruined
    religion. You ruined *tasawwuf*. You ruined *tariqa* and *silsilah*. You left
        nothing for us here but a ruin and a sign. The continued existence
        of this world seeks you and denounces you.
The end of this world in the fire of God's justice—justifies you.
I have had my fill of you, after only a sip—but your hunger and thirst
    for me, for the bread of my speech, the wine of my blood, the salt of
        my poverty, remains unsatisfied:
Understand by this the great difference in our two capacities.
That hunger fills my heart, casting out heaven and earth. It counts my
    breath, and rides it. It counts my bones, throwing them like dice on
        the platter. And then it slits my throat.

Other than that hunger, burning in the clefts of Sinai,
There is nothing left of me.
I am the ruins of the feast.
I am the cup that was broken before the wine was vinted, before the
  grapes were crushed and the vine planted, before the vineyard and its
  the earthen floor were laid.
I am the worthless coin that only Nothing can buy.
Since I first drew breath, my only name has been Nothing.
Since my last breath escaped me, my only word has been HE!
I will never have my fill of You—and if we hunger for You, it is only
  because Your own hunger is eternally satisfied, Your longing for
  infinite Beauty eternally fulfilled
In the embrace of Your own Beauty.
Islam is Your secret; I cannot even submit unless You will it.
The Qur'an is Your secret; my soul has no space upon it for even a
  single *alif.*
Whatever my destiny, the Garden or the Fire, my Heart already holds
  the entire text.
My self-love excludes me from You, until the day you make it die—and
  after that
It's your own Self-love that excludes me—this time forever. My one
  prayer
Is that some day it will exclude me absolutely,
So that no whining, starving wretch, hanging on your doorsill, will
  remain.
Your Absence is the sign of Your Presence and the root of my existence;
Your Presence is the proof of my annihilation.
If You are satisfied to live between the walls of my ruined house,
To found your throne on my eternal insufficiency, on the cold ashes of
  my struggle,
Then here's the deed and the bequest.

II: Seven Poems

Barzakh

If there were a dark night
In which darkness itself was visible,
What eye could see it?
If the Sun stepped out
Through night's curtains at midnight,
Then even before dawn
Night would be at an end
And dawn without a gate.
This is why, in His mercy
God gave the Moon to Muhammad:
As a law, a veil, and a warning.

The Salt of the Guide

I dove under the disks of the harrow;
I was torn by the blades, became one with
    the field—
And the Farmer who harrowed me
Was HE.

I lay beneath the surface of the water
Holding a hatchet in my right hand and
    another in my left—
And the Stag who stood above me
On the surface of the windy ocean
Was HE.

Hell cures us from Paradise, and Paradise
    from the fires of this world.
Quicksilver for an angry man, says the
    physician's art,
Brimstone for a fool—

But nothing crystallizes, the work is not
    complete
Until the missing ingredient is supplied:
The Salt of the Guide.

Under the Hammer

When you were at work in the quarry,
   breaking rocks
A willing slave, a king hid in a ruin
I went and lay down
Under the hammers of your remembrance.
What I had made of myself, you unmade
With the craft of the quarryman and the
   mason.

When you were at work in the smithy,
A coal black smith, face gone dark
From staring into the fire,
I went into the forge and lay down
Under the bellows of your remembrance.
Your face gave light
Till I reached white heat.

What refuge from the hammer, except
   on the anvil?
What refuge from the fire
But in the forge itself?
What does it matter if I become a cup or
   a blade, a stirrup or an axe-head
If I bear the stamp of the Master?

Separation

He is there
and I am here.
There is neither a path nor
a wall between us,
and I am paralyzed
by my own uselessness.
If you go to war against me,
my Friend,
with your great strength
I may somehow find the
strength to follow. . . .

—that's why I
taunt You.

Embracing the Fire

The Fire is kindled;
Hear it seethe and crackle.

Suffering is the Fire:
Dhikr fans the flames.

Dhikr is the Fire,
Suffering the fuel that feeds it.

My wandering attention
Lights like a fool on
This or that perishing thing—

Dhikr calls it home:
Home to the Fire.

My heart is the altar,
Dhikr the Fire,
My living flesh the sacrifice.

Every nest on this world's tree:
Thrown into the Fire.
No perch. No resting-place.
No home.

Don't let the Fire starve.
Never let it die.
Bring more suffering.
Bring more fuel.
What would not wish
To pass through that Fire
And become immortal?

Come, fear of death.
Come, terror of failure.

Come, grim loneliness.
Come, weight of the world.

To feel pain is to suffer;
To suffer is to bear;
To bear is to allow;
To allow is to prevail.

The Fire speaks the Name!
The Fire is the burning Name
Of Him Who speaks it.

Beaten on the anvil of it
I take the single shape
That is His will.
Sweet Fire. Pungent knowledge.
Fragrant wood-smoke
Leads the vigilant, listening world

Back to the Heart of the Fire.

Gratitude

Thank you, God, for being God.
Thank you for not leaving that job to me
To be the puppet of my own faithlessness,
An incompetent, fumbling creator
Who somehow knew how to make a world
But never learned how to govern it.
What I will do, You have already done;
Where I must fail, You can never fail.
That we don't all die the first time we
    fall asleep
But wake together in the common morning
As if we had never been obliterated
Is conclusive proof of both Your reality,
    and our need.
O God, thank you for the gift of my need.

Inside God

Inside God
    There is the sound of distant traffic,
    The smell of rose incense,
    And one cricket.

Inside God
    Somebody keeps leaving and returning
    With the rhythm of the breath.
    He was never really here,
    And so he never really left.

Inside God
    Someone is listening through the ear
    And things are listening to themselves.
    Across the marsh
    A young dog is barking.
    The cricket starts, then stops.

Inside God
    Everything becomes part of the world.
    No one is looking at the world,
    And yet this world is clearly seen.

Inside God
    The mystery that Someone could be
    Without starting waves
    Without making declarations
    Is the quality of the autumn wind,
    Of a truck changing gears,
    Of children playing.

A gap in the flow
    Of things naming themselves,
    The dog barking "*dog*,"
    The child screaming "*child*,"
    Is the place of the Name.

Here, He says, is the Friend you were searching for
    Looking out through your eyes
    Upon currents of laughter
    And motionless objects, somberly involved
    In the act of being.

He Who is no-one
    Is the very One
    Who lets all these things be.
    The cricket chirps "*God.*"

Inside God
    I was a small object seen on the horizon.

III: Nineteen Odes after Hafiz

Fifteen under the Sign of *Alif,*
Four under the Sign of *Ba*

"Transcreated" from the English Translation of H. Wilberforce Clarke

Alif

1

Bartender! Pass the pitcher.
Love seemed easy at first
But now, the bitter edge.

Because of the dizzying scent the breeze brushed loose
Just before dawn from that lock of hair
That twisted, musky curl
What blood shook the hearts of my friends!

Dye your prayer-rug with wine
If the Zoroastrian master commands it:
The one who has made the journey
Knows the route, and the milestones,
And the etiquette of the road.

At the kilometer of the Beloved
What joy I knew, and what relief
When the death-bell briefly spoke, and told me:
Pack your bags!

This dark night, this fear of the wave
And the terrible whirlpool—
How can those who left their burdens on the shore,
The ones who travel light—
How can they know our state?

My life's-work brought public shame
Because I followed my dream;
How can the mystery of love still remain a secret
When it's debated in public assemblies?

Hafiz! If you crave His presence
Then be present for *Him;*
When you visit your Beloved, leave the world behind:
Let it slip from your grasp.

2

The beautiful light of the Moon
Is from the light of a different face—

Your face.

The perfect dimple on that lovely chin—

it's Yours

Lord, when these desires arise
And come to sit beside us
Our hearts will be full and still,
While the windblown trees, still dishevelled—

they will be Yours.

My soul rises to my lips for sight of You.
It goes back, it comes again, it almost leaves me.
This fatal rhythm—

is it Yours?

When you pass beyond us,
Pass beyond the dust and the blood
Take care not to brush against us
With the hem of your skirt;
Too many of us have already become sacrificial victims—

Yours.

My heart destroys itself—go and bring this news
To one who still has a heart.
I swear it's true, my friends,
I swear by my soul, and by that other Soul—

                                                            Yours.

By the turning of Your eye, no-one got his rightful share
Of pleasure: better to strip off the veil of chastity
And sell it to the drunken ones—

                                                            Yours.

Then maybe our sleep-ruined luck will learn to pay
    attention
Because a bead of water at the corner of its eye
Reflected a shining face—

                                                            Yours!

Send me the wind, and along with it, gathered from the
    blush on your cheek,
Send handfuls of roses— then maybe I'll catch a whiff of
    fragrance
From the dust of the rose-garden—

                                                            Yours.

O winemasters at the feast of the gathered ones,
We wish you long life
Even if our cup still isn't full
When another cup is passed around—

                                                            Yours.

Passing breeze, bring this message from us
To the inhabitants of Yazd: Tell them to take command
Of those blind to the truth; make them like the ball
On the playing-field—

                                                            Yours.

Though we may be far from the field of nearness,

Our desire is not far; slaves of your King,
The praises we sing

                    are Yours.

O King of Kings, whose star is high, bless me for God's
    sake;
Like the sky, let me kiss the dust of that courtyard—

                    Yours.

Now Hafiz has a prayer to offer; listen, and say "amen":
Let those sweet, sugar-dripping lips of Yours
Be my daily bread

3

Bartender! With the light of wine set fire to the cup—

                    ours.

Musician! Convince us that the work of the world has
    been congenial to desire—

                    ours!

We have seen in the cup the reflection of the face of our
    Beloved:
Idiot! What can you know of the joys of perpetual
    drunkenness. . . .

                    ours?

The coy glances, the graceful movements of those willowy
    forms distracted us
Till the moment when, tall as the pine-tree,
The spear-like cypress-tree of Grace Itself walked in—

                    all ours.

The one whose heart is alive with love, that one
    never dies;

On the scroll of the world an everlasting existence is
    written:

                                                        ours.

I'm afraid there'll be no profit for us on the Day of
    Resurrection;
Better the lawful bread of the shaykh
Than this illicit water

                                                    of ours.

Breeze, if you happen to pass by the rose-bed of the
    beloveds
Be sure to take to that one beloved

                                    this message of ours:

Why have you deliberately stricken our name
From your memory? (That's what happens
When forgetfulness takes its place;
It finds no room for the face

                                        that once was ours.)

Our heart-enslaving Loved One loves to see us drunk:
That's why drunkenness has completely taken over the
    reins of life—

                                                        ours.

The turquoise sky and the ship of the new moon
Are drowned in the favor of that Haji Kivan

                                                    of ours.

My heart was caught, like the tulip in the cold air;
Bird of fortune, when will you fly into this snare

                                                    of ours?

Hafiz! Take care that your tears
Never stop falling; then, perhaps, the Bird of Union
will risk the trap—

                                            and be ours.

4

Come here, Sufi:
Because the mirror of the cup is bright
You can see the ruby light of the wine.

No-one hunts the Anka, so dismantle your trap;
Nothing remains in the hand of the snare
But the wind. Let your struggle live
In the pleasure of the moment, and remember:
When the well ran dry
Adam himself let go of the Garden and the house of
    safety.

At the banquet of time, have one for host, one for the road
And then go: perpetual union, here
Is not in the cards.

O heart! the strength of youth has gone
Before you could pick even one rose from the garden of
    life.
Hedonists, libertines,
Drunk as the Mystery that lies hidden in the veil,
For the elevated, self-denying ones
Your state is not becoming.

But as for us, hanging on your doorsill
We're yours to command.
Look again on your slave, Sir; take pity on him!

The day this heart placed its reins
In the hand of Your love,
I gave up the desire for an easy life.

I am the disciple of Jamshid's cup: I am Hafiz.
Breeze, take a greeting from this nameless slave
To the Shaikh of Jam.

5

Waiter. One more drink.
Throw your dust on the head
Of time's anguish.

Place the winecup in my hand
So I can strip this patched shirt of midnight blue
From my breast.

The wise call us notorious—
What do we want with their good opinion?

Bring wine! How long, tossed
In the wind of pride? How much dust on the head
Of useless desire?

When I sighed, the smoke of my blazing heart
Incinerated all the punks.

In high society, or in the gutter with the lowlife:
Not one friend of the secret
Of my ravaged heart.

Yet my heart is glad with a Comforter
Who once, from my heart, took comfort.

Whoever has seen the Silver Cypress
Will never set eyes on the cypress in the field again.

Patience in adversity, both day and night, Hafiz,
May bring you in the end to your desire.

6

For God's sake, pious ones!
My heart has flown from my hand—
Holy ones, for God's sake!
The pain of this mystery is begging to be revealed.

We are the ones whose boat is stranded.
Rise, wind! Then maybe once again
We'll behold the face of the Beloved.

The planets distribute their magic and sorcery
For no more than ten days;
Consider our friendship, O Friend, as your plunder.

Last night in the assembly of the rose and the wine
The bulbul sang deliciously:
Steward! Bring wine! Drunken ones—come to life!

The winecup is the mirror of Alexander:
Gaze into it and see the sorry state
Of the empire of Darius.

Generous One: In gratitude for your own safety
Maybe some day you'll inquire as to the welfare
Of this starving wretch
Of a darvish.

The comfort of the two worlds
Is in the meaning of these two words:
Kindness to friends; courtesy to enemies.

They refused to admit us
To the street of good reputation;
If you disagree with their decision,
Then change our fate.

This bitter wine, the one the Sufi called "mother of
     iniquities"
Is sweeter and more pleasant to us
Than the kisses of virgins.

When times are hard, go after pleasure;
See just how drunk you can get.
This potion of Existence makes a beggar rich as Karun.
But don't be arrogant, or the anger of the Heart-Ravisher
In whose hand even flint turns to wax
Will burn you out like a candle.

These lovely ones, whispering and giggling in the Persian
     tongue
Are the givers of life. Wine-steward,
Take news of this to the old men of Fars;

If the minstrel calls on the companions
Of this Persian lyric to dance,
It will attract those old men.

Hafiz didn't put on this patched and wine-stained robe
     all by himself;
O shaikh whose robe is clean,
Forgive our hopeless ways.

7

The splendor of youth has returned to the garden;
The good news of the rose has reached the bulbul;
His song is sweet.

Breeze, if you come again to the young men seated in
    the meadow,
Bring this prayer to the cypress, the rose and the sweet
    basil.

If the young Zoroastrian wine-seller reveals his glory
    openly,
I'll turn my eye-lash into a dust-broom
And sweep the dust at the
Door of his tavern.

When you draw the veil of black ambergris
Over the face of the Moon,
Don't drive me crazy; my head is spinning already.

The crowd jeers at us for drinking the dregs;
Am I afraid of them?
They will ruin their faith in the end.

Be the friend of the men of God, and remember:
There was a handful of dust in Noah's Ark
That wasn't interested in buying up the whole flood
For one drop of water.

Tell him whose last bed
Is two handfuls of earth: What interest do you still have
In building towers that reach to heaven?

Clear out of this house, whose roof is the sky,
And don't ask for bread:
The dark cup, in the end, always kills the guest.

That Moon of Canaan, that Throne of Egypt is yours:
It's time to tell your prison-house good-bye!

What plot do you keep in the tip of your curl
That makes you let down, once more, the flood
Of that perfumed hair?
If your head keeps spinning in the circle of what *might* be,
You will never begin to know the mysteries
Of what *must* be.

The kingdom of liberty, and somewhere within it, a little
    corner of contentment
Is a prize the Sultan himself can't take with the sword.

Drink wine, Hafiz, and practice dissipation. Be happy.
But don't, in your happiness— like some others have—
Turn the Holy Qur'an
Into your snare of deceit.

8

If that Turk of Shiraz takes my heart,
I'll give Bokhara and Samarkand both for the mole on
    her cheek.

Steward! Bring out what's left of the wine.
In Paradise you will have neither the grassy bank of the
    Ruknabad
Nor the rose in Musalla's garden.

These sweet, teasing workers, the torment of the city
Steal patience from the heart, just like the Turks
Lift tribute from the tray.

What does the Beloved's beauty
Need with our own flawed beauty?

Loveliness Itself requires neither makeup, nor rouge,
Nor painted mole, nor pencilled eyebrow.

When I saw that every day Joseph became more beautiful,
I knew that love for him would bring out Zulaikha
From behind the curtain of virginity.

Sing the story of troubadour and wine,
Forget trying to catch the mystery of time.
No-one has ever solved it, with all the skill at their
     command;
And you will fail too.

You insulted me, and I was happy;
Now that you've taken to flattering me,
May God Almighty forgive you.
Bitter words are more appropriate
Coming from that red, succulent, sugar-greedy lip.

You strung pearls on the thread of the night when you
     sang that lyric;
Maybe, if Hafiz sings sweetly enough,
The thread will break—scatter the constellation
Of the Pleiades.

9

Speak softly, breeze, to that lovely gazelle;
Tell him it's all because of him
That we dream of steep mountains, of barren deserts.

The sugar-merchant—may he enjoy long life—
Never asks the fate
Of the parrot who eats his sugar.

When you sit next to the Beloved, drinking wine,
Remember, sometimes, those others you have loved

Whose job is to measure it out.

Rose! Why don't you ask
What ever became of your nightingale?
But I suppose your great beauty
Does not permit of such distractions.

A sweet disposition can catch a cunning bird
Better than a net or trap—whoever has real insight
Knows this.

Why is it that those dark-eyed, statuesque beauties
With faces like the full moon
Never wear the color
Of constancy?

There is no defect in your beauty, except this one:
That the loveliness of that face can never be divided
Between love, and constancy.

When luck is your friend,
When you're there with all your friends,
When gratitude overcomes you,
Take that opportunity to remember us—
Transients of the desert and the plain.
Look up at the sky— imagine!
What if the lyrics of Hafiz, and the singing of Zahra
Brought Jesus the Messiah
Dancing on the clouds of heaven?

10

Our Pir abandoned the mosque last night
And headed for the tavern instead!
Now what should his poor disciples do?
How can we face toward the Kaaba
When our Teacher can't face in any direction at all
Except toward the Winemaster?
I suppose we'll have to take up residence
In the Tavern of the Fire-worshipper;
That must have been our destiny
Since before the beginning of time.

Locked in that lock,
In the hangman's noose of that dark hair,
His heart is happy.
(The wise would lose their minds
If wisdom only knew.)

One day, my heart
Caught the bird of peace in its snare—
Then, you let down your hair.
Unaware of the trembling of my hand,
I let the bird go.

When I saw the beauty of your face
Suddenly I understood the meaning of a verse of the
    Qur'an
That had long eluded me:
Ever since that night, grace and beauty
Have been the whole of my exegesis.

What has one night
Of sighs raining like fire—
What has the fire of the heart
Burning in the blackness of one night ever accomplished
Against the stone of your heart?

When the wind ruffled the mass of your hair,
The world before me turned black.
Passion for that hair of yours (to speak of anything further
Would dishonor me)
Shot my sigh like an arrow
Across the border of the sky.
Have mercy on your soul, Hafiz. Keep silent.
Avoid the arrow of your friends.
Since our Pir has turned into a drunkard,
I'll sleep every night in the doorway of his tavern—
Like Hafiz.

11

Who will bring this prayer to the friends of the King:
"If you are grateful for your sovereignty
Then don't drive the beggar from your sight"?

From the demon Watcher, lodged in the soul of man
I take refuge in God,
Praying for a little help from His light.

When your face turns to fire, Beloved,
You burn the whole world.
What good can come to you from such cruelty?
What is this turbulence you display to your lovers—
You, bright as the Moon, tall as the Cypress?

All night I wait in hope
That the dawn-breeze will bring the one message
Destined for every lover
To *this* lover.

If your dark eyelash has lusted for my blood, O Idol,
What deceit! If you must shoot,
Then shoot straight!

From the deception of that sorcerer's eye
My whole heart has turned to blood.
See how your eye has killed me—see it!

O Guide! That lover who rises up before dawn,
For God's sake hand him the cup;
His morning prayer
May do you some good.

The heart of Hafiz, broken by separation, is filled with
    blood—
God only knows what blood might rise
If Union came!

12

The "dignity of labor"—where is it?
And me, my life now ruined—where am I?
Between this "where" and that
How long is the Path!

What possible connection can there be
Between this debauchery and that rectitude?
The heeding of moral exhortation—where is it?
The wild song of the lute—where is *that*?
My heart is bone-tired of the monastery, and the patched
    cloak of hypocrisy.
Where is the temple of the Magi?
Where is the pure wine?

He's gone. I hope the time of union
Will be to him, at least, a pleasant memory.
That indulgent glance, that hard reproof—
Where are they now?

From the face of the Friend what profit came
To the black hearts of his enemies?

Where are those dead lamps without him?
Where is the radiant candle of the Sun?

We're using the dust of your threshold to paint our eyes
    with.
Where do we go now? Toward "the well-ordered life?"
Wonderful advice! But *where?*

A word to the wise: Never let your wandering eye
Come to rest on that dimpled chin—it's a pit
At the center of the road.

Where are you off to now, my heart?
Your haste is admirable, but do you really have a
    destination?
Don't expect either ease or patience from Hafiz, my friend.
Ease—what's that? Patience? Never heard of it.
Sleep . . . where is it?

    It's gone.

13

We all turned out, that day, to see you off.
You alone, who know our hearts, know our grief,
How bad luck has plundered all our sustenance.

But now, scattering tears, we're sprinkled with gold-dust
Like your hair when it's netted with jewels
From the joy your messenger brought us
When he placed your letter in our hand.

In prayer, I come before you; I hope that you also
Will extend your hands in prayer:
Mine, that you be renowned for your fidelity;
Yours, that God help us to endure your absence.

I swear by your head
That if every sword in this world were to split open my
    head
The world could never extract from this head of ours
The desire for your face.

The turning sky has made me an aimless wanderer, and
    you know why:
It's jealous of our friendship.
If every soul in the world were to oppress you,
Our Lord would call out justice from every soul in this
    world
To vindicate you.

The day may come again
When our beloved will return to us in safety;
O happy day, when the beloved, in security
Shall enter my house.

When we sang of that downy cheek and its loveliness,
The rose-leaf herself blushed when she read
The leaves of this book.
To those who claim that Hafiz
Has made only short journeys, I answer:
The length of this single journey
Has never removed its steady, forward-gazing head
From that spinning head of ours.

14

If you choose not to hide your face from beggars,
That will be grace.

Obedient, then, to the Heart's desire
Our eye will behold your face.

Like angel Harut, we live in love's devastation;
We wish our eye

Had never seen that face!
Slave to the dimple in your chin
What would have become of angel Harut
If a trace of your beauty had not been whispered
To angel Marut?

The rose gave out its perfume—just as if, O Peri,
You placed your footsteps in the meadow where it grew.
If our eye had glimpsed your face in that one moment
We would be drunk as nightingales.

Blood-thirsty idol! The tyranny of your absence
Slits our throat. Be courteous to us at least once before we
    die;
Unveil your face
To Hafiz!

15

Ever since Your beauty called Your lovers to Union
They have fallen into calamity, heart and soul
From that curling tress, that night-dark mole.

What the souls of Your lovers have endured through
    separation
Is known to no-one else—
Except for those heroes who knew the selfsame thirst
On the field of Karbala!

If that Brazen One now practices drunkenness and debauchery,
To give up chastity and asceticism, O my soul
Is our moral duty.

The hour of pleasure, the season of joy, the days of wine
    and roses—
One raid plundered them all. They were nothing but five
    days' free time

Between one job and the next.

If kissing the King's foot does you any good, Hafiz,
All grandeur and dignity and sublimity will be yours
In this world and the next.

Ba

16

"O King of Beauty," I said
"Take pity on this penniless stranger."
"By following his own heart's desire," he said,
"The wretched stranger loses his way."

"Then travel along with me," I said, "at least for a
    little while."
"I must decline," he said—
"What does the pampered homebody care
For the sorrows of some penniless stranger?"

That coddled, pampered one, bedded in ermine like
    a king—
What grief for him if some stranger
Should turn his couch to a thorn, his pillow to
    a stone!
In the ropes of your hair the souls of so many lovers
    are tangled and caught;
That this musky beauty-mark
Should fall on your painted cheek—how strange.

Strange that your face is lined with down
Like a fine trail of ants, searching for your image;
Yet in the gallery of the masterpiece
That dark, fragrant outline
Is in no way strange.

In the mirror of your moon-like face
The glow of wine is reflected,
Like the red leaf of the Arghavan on the petal of the
    wild rose—
Strange.

"O night-dark tress" I cried, "O evening of the
    stranger!"
"Watch out, then, stranger," he said;
"When morning comes, I will listen to no complaints."

"O rising Moon! Never hide those rosy cheeks—
If you do, you will turn me into an
Exhausted, destitute stranger."

"If even my friends, Hafiz
Are astonished at my beauty,
When a perfect stranger lies distraught and shattered before me,
Who could call that strange?"

17

The morning blossoms, and immediately the cloud conceals it
    under her veil.
The cup of the morning, my friends! The morning cup!

The face of the tulip is withered
In the grip of the frost—wine, my friends! Bring wine!

From the meadow the breeze of Paradise is blowing,
So drink pure wine—without pause, without end.

The rose has set her emerald throne in the center of the
    meadow—
Bring wine red as ruby, wine red as fire!

The tavern door, again they've closed it—

Open it for us, you Opener of Doors!
It's amazing how quickly they rush to close it,
And always at a time like this!
Your ruby lip holds the rights of salt
Against those whose wounded hearts
Are roasted on a spit;

Let the ascetic drink wine like the reveler;
Let the wise fear God.

If your quest is for the water of life
Then drink sweet wine to the sound of the harp;

If you boldly seek for life like Alexander,
Then take as your trophy
The crimson lip of the Beloved.

To the memory of the Saki, formed like the youths of
    Paradise
Drink pure wine in the season of the rose.

Don't grieve, Hafiz; your fortune has been told:
Some day the Beloved will lift for you
The corner of the veil.

18

The morning of good fortune has come!
Where is the bowl, beaten and burnished like the sun?
Bring the cup quickly, for opportunity knocks.

In this house without strife, the Cupbearer is my friend
And subtle wisdom flows
From the minstrel's lips.

It is the season of youth, the hour of ease;
From hand to hand, the cup goes round.

This cup of gold was mixed with the ruby elixir
Only to expand the heart, to adorn it with the jewel
Of beauty and gladness.

The drunken ones are dancing, the Beloved and his
    minstrel are waving their arms
In time to the music;
The Saki has stolen sleep from every eye.

This house of safety, this secret cell, this hidden chamber
    of pleasure
Where best friends meet—
Whoever has found his way into our company
Has found the locked and guarded house
Where a hundred doors stand open.

Thinking to add even further grace to the essence of wine
The subtle breeze, Nature's coutourier
Placed rose-water in the leaf of the rose.

When I knew that the Full Moon had paid with his soul for
    those pearls of Hafiz,
In that very moment, the sharp twang of the lute
Touched the ear of Zuhra!

19

The Gardens of Paradise draw life from the Garden of Union;
From the tortures of separation, one burning drop
Kindles all the fires of Hell.

Paradise and the Lote Tree have taken shelter
Beneath the luster of your cheek, the grace of your stature.
A good home for them, and a joyous homecoming!

All night the river of Paradise gazes, as my own eye gazes, upon
    your intoxicated Eye;

In every season, the name of your beauty is Spring;
In every book, the name of your grace is Paradise.

My heart was consumed before ever reaching its desire;
If my heart had reached the goal it would never have poured out
 its heart's blood before you.

Your lip and mouth hold sovereign rights
Over how many torn livers, how many roasted hearts?

Don't think that your lovers are only to be found in the circle
 of your friends;
How many lone ascetics, too, are crazy with love for you?
But the news of them has never reached you.

By the curl of your lip
I knew that the buried luster of the ruby was smelted
By the world-illuminating sun.

How long will you hide behind modesty? Open your veil!
What treasure are you hiding beneath it
Except your modesty?

The rose saw your face and toppled into the fire;
It smelled your fragrance and, for shame, turned into rosewater.

For love of your face, Hafiz is drowned in the sea of catastrophe;
Come to him! Help him! He's breathing his last!

Hafiz—don't let your life pass in foolishness;
Remember that breath is precious, and try hard!

IV: Five Prophets
In Light of the *Fusus al-Hikam*

Abraham

If you were not my Secret,
How could I ever have found you,
Among the tents?

If I were not your own Secret, jealously guarded,
How could I ever have submitted
To being called Your friend?

When I knew myself alone,
Exiled from the world,
I discovered your secret Name
Inscribed on the Guarded Tablet.

When I emerged from that solitude,
To lose myself in tribes and armies,
You felt my loss.
You searched for me everywhere,
Found me in my exile,
And named me Your friend.

At Your command I raised my right hand
To slay my only son—
I looked again, and he was Thou.
I dropped the knife.

When we sat together on a cushion of grass
Inside the Walled Garden of the Mysteries,
Eating from our own vine and fig tree
And talking to our heart's content,
The desert, shimmering white and yellow
On the horizon beyond us
Stood in need of the clear Arabic tongue.

In love you led me
Into the barren places of the earth.
In anger you drove me, with slaps and bitter words
Toward the chamber of Night
Where you were waiting for me already,
Watching over my sleep,
The rising and falling of my breast,
Till the mazes of the stars and the night of time
Passed over, and the morning came.

Noah and Adam

The Prophet Noah overthrew the idols:
Grotesque statues with the heads of animals.
The sea of space and time closed over them.

Noah rode the flood
On the Ark of the Human Form,
Surrounded by all the animals, two by two,
In Beauty and Majesty.
And the ribs of the Prophet Adam
Were the timbers of that ship.

Before sun and moon and stars were made,
Adam, by God's command,
Recited the Names
Of the beasts and their angels.
As the generations rose,
Hunting beasts for meat and
Naming them for power,
God sent the Prophet Noah to remind us
That no beast possesses his own name
Or knows how to speak it.

When the forms of other-than-God
Are drowned in the flood,
Then the Names of God are gathered,
And Man—hidden form of the Formless
Secret word of the Silence—
Is their Book and their Ark.

Moses Complains of Torah

Her generosity to many was her wrath;
   her cruelty to me, her mercy.
Though she played the Pharaoh
   in the tyranny of her beauty,
She required me to be Moses,
   and walk the narrow path.

⊕

[If Moses had come down from Sinai without Torah,
He would have burned to ashes the Children of Israel.]

Salih

The prophet Salih bought a she-camel from
    God—
The Tribe of Thamud hamstrung it.
But didn't both tribe and camel drink from
    the same well?
The Tribe of Thamud feasted for three days
Until God's Shout destroyed them in their
    tents.
But wasn't Salih the one who led that camel
    to slaughter in the first place?
And were the Tribe of Thamud liable to God's
    judgment
Before the prophet Salih broke in upon their
    sleep?
If the elements had not risen up against God
He could never have created them; by His
    world-creating Shout
He destroyed them in their rebellious non-entity,
And sent them out, His willing slaves, into the
    mountains and deserts of this world.
Whatever departs from God, said the prophet
    Salih
Is most surely on its way to Him.

AFTERWORD & INVITATION:
COURSE IN HIGH POETRY

Dear Reader:

This book actually forms one-fourth of a course of study in "High Poetry"—the poetic art as it was, and might conceivably be again, when practiced from the standpoint of the Primordial Tradition that produced Homer, Dante, Wolfram von Eschenbach, Milton, Blake, Shakespeare, Rumi, Hafiz, Chandidas, Kalidasa, Han Shan, Whitman, Emily Dickinson, and so many others. (Reader take note: certainly not all of my own poetry fits this description; I can only hope that some of it might climb that peak from time to time.) The other three-fourths of that course are represented by my books *Folk Metaphysics: Mystical Meanings in Traditional Folk Songs and Spirituals* and *Who Is the Earth? How to See God in the Natural World*, as well as by *Shadow of the Rose: The Esoterism of the Romantic Tradition*, this last co-authored with my wife, Jennifer Doane Upton.

Only *The Wars of Love* and *Folk Metaphysics* are devoted to poetry as such; the other two deal, in a not-unpoetic way, and often illustrated by quoted verse, with the metaphysics of Nature and Romance respectively, and thus with the essential principles that underlie all Pastoral and Romantic poetry—using "pastoral" in its widest sense to denote all types of verse that render the beauty or majesty or simple homely ways of the natural world, from Keats to Issa to Robinson Jeffers, and "romantic" as covering both the kind of human love that takes us beyond ourselves, as in the Arthurian romance *Sir Gawain and the Green Knight*, and the passionate, impossible love for God Himself such as Jalalluddin Rumi sang.

In these four books I do my best to demonstrate, from four differing standpoints, exactly how High Poetry transcends both the identity and role of the "individual genius" (not to mention the individual arrogant nihilistic nobody), and also leaves gratefully behind the whole regime of *self-expression*, that cramped, narrow house that such "geniuses" have elected to spend their lives in (and which, as is proved by this book, I am not totally free of myself). In the world of High Poetry, *mythopoesis* is revealed as the "symbolist" expression of metaphysics, just as metaphysics is shown to be, in many ways, the philosophical hermeneutic of mythopoesis. Through the eagle eye of High Poetry we can see just how the poetic art at its best, when married to the objectivity and detachment and death-to-self that metaphysics rigorously requires and also mercifully provides, might yet let us live in a world where the words of W. B. Yeats, from his poem "Among School Children", describe the actual quality of vision:

> Labour is blossoming or dancing where
> The body is not bruised to pleasure soul,
> Nor beauty born out of its own despair,
> Nor blear-eyed wisdom out of midnight oil.

If you are interested in further dialogue or even tutelage on subjects such as these, first buy and read my other three books, and then feel free to contact me through Sophia Perennis.

Sincerely,
Charles Upton

RSVP

P.S. A recitation by the author of his short epic *The Wars of Love* is available as a CD. If you are interested, inquire at cupton@qx.net.

www.ingramcontent.com/pod-product-compliance
Lightning Source LLC
Chambersburg PA
CBHW021357090426
42742CB00009B/892